Understanding Accounting Fundamentals:
The Logic of Debit/Credit

Francis A. Bird, Ph.D., CPA
Professor of Accounting, Emeritus
The University of Richmond

ISBN- 1453829393

Far more knowledge results from exploring why
a set of conditions exists than from simply accepting
those conditions and committing them to memory.

How the States Got Their Shapes,
Mark Stein © 2008
HarperCollins Publishers

Preface

In the course of thirty years of teaching accounting, it has been my observation that many, if not most, beginning accounting students rely on memorization to learn accounting fundamentals. To me, this is unfortunate since it amounts to learning in a vacuum, i.e., without an awareness of the conceptual underpinnings of debit/credit accounting. With this in mind, the book begins by explaining why double-entry accounting exists and what its underlying concepts are. Then the logic stemming from these concepts is used throughout the book to explain how debit/credit procedures are implemented and how the financial statements result. In short, the objective of the book is to have the reader learn accounting through logical conceptual reasoning and application as opposed to rote memorization.

Organizationally, the book begins in *Chapter One* by identifying and explaining the underlying accounting concepts of entity, exchange, reclassification, revenue, cost, expense, and owner's equity. These basic ideas and the logic they impart are then used in *Chapters Two* through *Four* in an example of accounting for a business entity over a two-year time period. *Chapters Five* and *Six* then cover some additional areas not covered in the business example. Exercises are provided at the end of each of the six chapters, and it is quite important to work through them to solidify understanding of the chapter material.

Admittedly, the impetus for the book was the desire to provide a self-help aid for beginning accounting students. The book achieves this and is compatible with all introductory accounting textbooks. It would make an excellent supplement to any one of them. The book is also eminently suitable as a stand-alone learning resource for anyone desiring an understanding of the double-entry debit/credit process of accounting.

In conclusion, a collective debt of gratitude is expressed to the several writers whose works are cited in the end notes to the book. In particular, appreciation is extended to Dr. William J. Schrader of the Pennsylvania State University for his inspiration and contributions in the area of inductive accounting theory. Appreciation is also expressed to Carol E. Matthews without whose help, this book would not have been possible.

Francis A. Bird

Forward

Before the book begins, a few comments will be made about the balance sheet equation. It is safe to say that the balance sheet equation is almost universally used as the basis for introductory accounting instruction. Students at the outset of the first course in accounting are told the equation is a "basic concept of accounting" and its rules are to be used for recording business "transactions and other events." However, the problem here is that qualitative definitions of "transactions and events" are not normally provided. In other words, the subject matter being recorded is ill-defined as to its inherent nature. This raises the following unanswered question: In general terms, what is it about that which is recorded that causes the balance sheet equation to exist? Or put a different way: What is the logic behind the debit/credit rules of the balance sheet equation? Answering these questions is one of the main purposes and goals of this book.

Contents

Chapter One

BASIC CONCEPTS
Exchange: Entity, Debit and Credit; Cost: Expense, Asset,
Reclassification; Revenue; Claims and Obligations:
Receivables, Payables, Owners' Equity.

Chapter Two

ACCOUNTS AND RECORDING
Journal and Ledger: Accounts, Journal Entries, Posting,
Balances.

Chapter Three

FINANCIAL STATEMENTS
Financial Statements: Trial Balance, Income Statement,
Statement of Retained Earnings, Balance Sheet; Closing
Entries; Journal Entry Effects: Statement Articulation,
Appendix: The Balance Sheet Equation

Chapter Four

COMPREHENSIVE EXAMPLE
Journal and Ledger: Journal Entries and Effects, Merchandise
Inventory, Income Taxes, Dividends, Trial Balance; Income
Statement and Balance Sheet: Classified Balance Sheet; Cash
Flow Statement: Indirect Method; Closing Entries; Appendix A: Periodic
Inventory Method; Appendix B: The Matching Concept;
Appendix C: Cash Flow Statement: Direct Method

Chapter Five

OTHER EXCHANGES AND ACCOUNTS I
Accruals and Prepayments: Accrued Expense and Revenue.
Prepaid Expense and Unearned Revenue; Gains and Losses: Lost Costs, Sales of Fixed Assets,
Debt Settlement, Trilateral Exchanges, Income Statement Content.

Chapter Six

OTHER EXCHANGES AND ACCOUNTS II
Contra and Adjunct Accounts: Sales Discounts, Uncollectible
Accounts, Accumulated Depreciation, Bond Discount and
Premium, Bond Redemption, Paid-in-Capital in Excess of Par, Deficit; Contractual Exchanges:
Executory Contracts, Levels of Exchange; Appendix: Current Value Reporting.

Chapter One
Basic Concepts

Exchange

One of the most fundamental concepts of accounting is <u>exchange</u> since it provides the basis for understanding why the debit/credit rules of accounting exist. It is the <u>exchange</u> transactions of a designated business <u>entity</u> which constitute the basic data accountants record and process into financial statements. In these exchanges, the entity <u>receives</u> something of value from another party and concurrently <u>gives</u> something of value to the other party. Note that the other party to the exchange can be either a non-owner or owner of the business since, for accounting purposes, the business entity is considered to be separate and distinct from its owners. An entity's exchange can be depicted as follows:

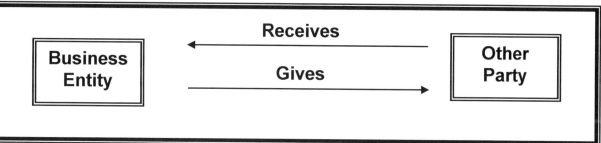

When recording the exchange, the accountant <u>debits</u> what the entity <u>receives</u>, and <u>credits</u> what the entity <u>gives</u>.[I*] Also, the agreed upon monetary value of the exchange is recorded with the same amount being entered for both the debit and credit. Assuming an amount of $100, the general form of an exchange recording in what is known as a <u>journal entry</u> is:

Dr:	**What is Received**	**$100**	
	Cr:	**What is Given**	**$100**

In the above entry, it is interesting to note two things. First, the abbreviation used for debit is dr. and for credit is cr. The reason for this is the abbreviations are the first and last letters of the words <u>debitor</u> and <u>creditor</u>, which were used in medieval Italian bank accounting to indicate receiver and giver respectively. The second interesting feature of the journal entry is the entering of the debit (received) on the left and the credit (given) on the right. As a matter of conjecture, this could be because most people are right handed, and in an exchange, the tendency of a right handed person would likely be to give with the right hand and receive with the left, if both actions were performed simultaneously.

There are four general types of things of value which can be transferred in exchanges.[II] These are:

1. Goods or Service
2. Cash
3. Claims against others
4. Obligations to others

Exchanges of the above value items will be examined in the remainder of this chapter.

Cost

Cost is a term accountants use in connection with the receipt of goods or services in an exchange, and it is used in two different senses. One author has discussed this dual use of the term cost as follows:

> "In his book, Economic Thought and Language, Professor Fraser of Aberdeen University points out that the word 'cost' is commonly used in two senses. He designates one concept as 'embodied costs', the other as 'displacement costs'. Embodied costs are the technical factors of production which go into the making of an article—the units of material, hours of labor, and units of energy used in producing it and thereby incorporated or embodied in it.
>
> Displacement costs, in contrast, are what is given up for something, not what goes into it. The displacement cost of having some heavy bags carried by a porter would be the fifty cents paid him. The embodied cost [received] would be the time and energy which the porter devoted to the service."[III]

To summarize: embodied costs are the goods or services received,[IV] while displacement costs are what is given to acquire those goods or services.

When goods or services (the embodied costs) are received, they are recorded in one of two ways depending on whether or not the goods or services have already been utilized (consumed) in the operations of the business. If they have been utilized, they are considered expired and labeled expenses. The general form of the accounting entry to record an expense exchange is:

Dr:	**Goods or Service Expense**	**$xxx**
	(utilized goods or service received,	
	the expired embodied cost)	
Cr:	**What is given**	**$xxx**
	(usually Cash or a Payable obligation,	
	the displacement cost)	

Normally, it is services such as those received from employees, utility companies, etc. which are debited to expense when received. Although, in some cases, goods received can be legitimately recorded by a debit to expense at the time of receipt. For example, small amounts of low value, short-lived office supplies would be debited to expense as purchased.

In contrast to expired goods or service expenses, unexpired goods or service received have not yet been utilized in the operations of the business. Such unexpired goods or service constitute one type of asset which can be held by a business entity. (There are two other types of assets: cash and claims against others.) The general form of the exchange entry for the acquisition of an unexpired goods or service asset is:

Dr:	**Goods or Service Asset**	**$xxx**
	(goods or service received,	
	the unexpired embodied cost)	
	Cr: **What is given**	**$xxx**
	(usually Cash or a Payable obligation,	
	the displacement cost)	

Normally, it is goods (i.e., tangible resources) such as land, buildings, equipment, and inventory which are debited to unexpired cost assets when received. Although, in some cases, services received are debited to assets. For example, in manufacturing operations the cost of factory labor service received would be debited to the assets produced as a part of their total cost of production.

Eventually an unexpired cost asset will become expired through its utilization in the operations of the entity. When this occurs, its expiration is recorded by making a reclassification[V] entry to transfer the unexpired goods or service cost or portion thereof, from asset to expense. This is done in the following manner.

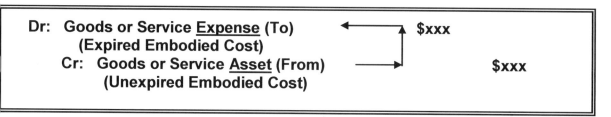

A short decision tree can help summarize and clarify the preceding ideas.

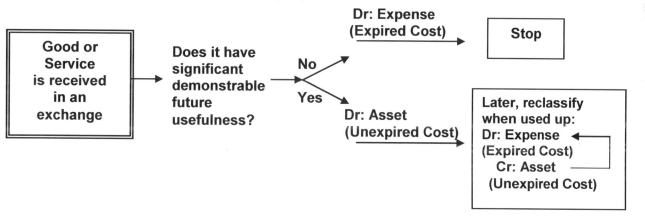

Reclassification entries, such as the one shown above for conversion of a good or service asset to expense, do not record new exchanges; they simply re-categorize old ones. That is, they transfer all or part of the amount of a previously recorded exchange out of one category and into another. Therefore, the entity's accounting record is still entirely composed of its exchange data.

Reclassification entries can take one of two general forms. The form of an entry for a reclassification of a previously recorded debit item (as in the case illustrated above) is:

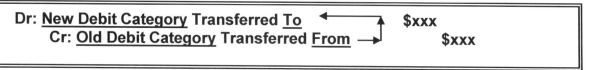

Most reclassification entries are of the type just illustrated which involves transferring a previously recorded <u>debit</u> item to <u>another debit</u> category. However, transferal of a previously recorded <u>credit</u> item to <u>another credit</u> category is also sometimes encountered. The general form of the entry for such a reclassification is:

Dr: <u>Old Credit Category</u> Transferred <u>From</u>   **$xxx**
    Cr: <u>New Credit Category</u> Transferred <u>To</u>   **$xxx**

When faced with a situation calling for a reclassification entry, the facts in the case would indicate the category to be "transferred from" and the category to be "transferred to". The proper categories to debit and credit can then be ascertained from this information.

<u>Revenue</u>

Revenue is a term accountants use in connection with the giving of goods and services, and, like cost, it is used in two different senses. Think back to the previous example of the porter carrying bags for a fee. It is repeated here for reference.

> "The <u>displacement cost</u> [given]of having some bags carried by a porter would be the fifty cents paid him. The <u>embodied cost</u> [received] would be the time and energy which the porter devoted to the service." [VI]

Note that the above quote is from the standpoint of <u>the one receiving the service</u>. Now consider the quote from the standpoint of <u>the porter giving the service</u>. From that vantage point the quote would read as follows:

> The <u>acquisition revenue</u> of having some bags carried by a porter would be the fifty cents he <u>received</u>. The <u>embodied revenue</u> would be the time and energy which the porter devoted to the service <u>given</u>.

This dual usage of the term revenue is discussed by Hendriksen in his <u>Accounting Theory</u> as follows:

> "Two approaches to the concept of revenue can be found in the literature, one focusing on the inflow of assets resulting from the operational activities of the firm and the other focusing on the creation of goods and services by the enterprise and the transfer of these to consumers or other producers. That is, revenue is considered to be either an inflow of net assets [acquisition revenue] or an outflow of goods and services [embodied revenue]." [VII]

To summarize: <u>acquisition revenues</u> are what is <u>received</u> for goods or services given, while <u>embodied revenues</u> are the goods and services <u>given</u>. [VIII]

Following the above train of thought, the general form of a revenue entry is:

> **Dr:** **What is <u>received</u>**   **$xxx**
> **(usually Cash or a Receivable claim,**
>   **the acquisition revenue)**
>   **Cr:**   **Goods or Service <u>Revenue</u>**   **$xxx**
>   **(goods or service <u>given</u>,**
>   **the embodied revenue)**

By way of summarization, the following illustration shows the overall parallelism present in cost and revenue entries.

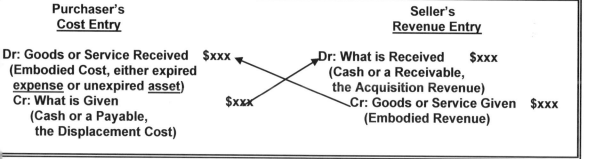

Claims and Obligations

Most of the preceding discussion has been devoted to cost and revenue. Before leaving this chapter, we also need to examine more closely the recording of claims (receivables), obligations to non-owners (payables), and the term "owner's equity". To further illustrate receivable and payable exchanges, a situation will be assumed in which one entity borrows cash from another with repayment to be made later. (Interest will be ignored for simplicity.) The appropriate journal entries are shown below. The arrows are included to show the parallelism between the entries.

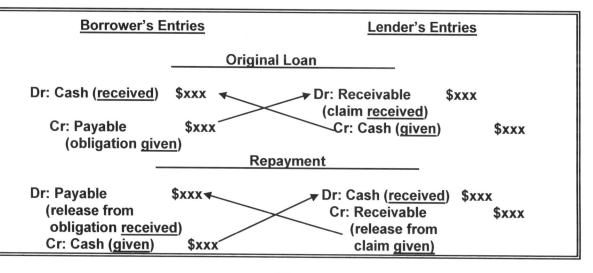

Finally, the term "owner's equity" needs clarification. Owner's Equity is usually defined as the owner's interest in, or claim against, the business entity. However, this definition is from the owner's viewpoint. From the entity's viewpoint, owner's equity is its obligation to the owner(s). This obligation view of owner's equity is supported in the literature by several authors. For example, Paton in his Accounting Theory states:

> "The entity has both fixed and contractual [payable] obligations to non-owner creditors and elastic and residual [owners' equity] obligations to owners"[IX]

And Gilman in his Accounting Concepts of Profit points out:

> "The accountant may and frequently does, conceal that element of his working philosophy which baldly asserts that an artificial entity owes money to a proprietor for his investment and accumulated profits. But this may be due to no lack of faith. Rather, it may be prompted by the desire to avoid legal arguments [about the legal status of the obligation]."[X]

As a brief illustration of accounting for owner's equity, assume an owner invests cash in a business entity, and subsequently the entity returns some cash to the owner. The journal entries for the entity would be:

---

1. Cash received from owner

Dr: Cash (received)	$xxx	
Cr: Owner's Equity		$xxx
(obligation given		
to owner)		

2. Cash returned to owner

Dr: Owner's Equity	$xxx	
(release from obligation		
to owner received)		
Cr: Cash (given)		$xxx

In this chapter, the basic concepts underlying debit/credit accounting were presented in general terms. In subsequent chapters, these ideas will be used in a more specific manner to implement the basic accounting process. But before going on, be sure to work through the two exercises which follow. The solutions follow the exercises.

Exercise 1 Basic Ideas

With words selected from the following list, fill in the blanks in the numbered statements which follow. (Hint: For help on items 3 to 11 refer to the journal entries shown in the chapter).

> Received
> Given
> Left
> Right
> Cash
> Receivable
> Goods Asset
> Payable
> Owners' Equity
> Revenue
> Expense

1. In recording an exchange, the <u>debit</u> records what is_____ and the <u>credit</u> what is_____.

2. In a journal entry, the <u>debit</u> would be placed on the _____ and the <u>credit</u> on the _____.

3. When <u>services</u> are <u>received</u> for a <u>cash</u> payment <u>given</u>, the <u>debit</u> is normally to _____ and the <u>credit</u> is to _____.

4. When <u>goods</u> are <u>received</u> and an <u>obligation</u> to a vendor is <u>given</u>, the <u>debit</u> is normally to _____ and the <u>credit</u> is to a _____.

5. When a <u>release from the obligation</u> to the vendor in 4 is <u>received</u> because <u>cash</u> is <u>given</u>, the <u>debit</u> is to a _____ and the <u>credit</u> is to _____.

6. When the usefulness of the goods purchased in 4 expires, a reclassification entry would be made which would <u>debit</u> _____ and <u>credit</u> _____.

7. When <u>cash</u> is <u>received</u> from a customer for <u>services given</u>, the <u>debit</u> is to _____ and the <u>credit</u> is to_____.

8. When a <u>claim</u> against a customer is <u>received</u> for <u>services given</u>, the <u>debit</u> is to a _____ and the <u>credit</u> is to _____.

9. When <u>cash</u> is <u>received</u> from the customer in 8 and a <u>release from the claim</u> is <u>given</u>, the <u>debit</u> is to _____ and the <u>credit</u> is to a _____.

10. When a business entity <u>receives cash</u> as an investment from owners and <u>gives an obligation</u> to them, the <u>debit</u> is to _____ and the <u>credit</u> is to _____.

11. When the business entity in 10 <u>receives a release from its obligation</u> to owners because it <u>gives</u> <u>cash</u> to them, the <u>debit</u> is to _____ and the <u>credit</u> is to _____.

Exercise 1 Solution

1. Received; Given

2. Left; Right

3. Debit Expense; Credit Cash

4. Debit Goods Asset; Credit Payable

5. Debit Payable; Credit Cash

6. Debit Expense; Credit Goods Asset

7. Debit Cash; Credit Revenue

8. Debit Receivable; Credit Revenue

9. Debit Cash; Credit Receivable

10. Debit Cash; Credit Owners' Equity

11. Debit Owners' Equity; Credit Cash

Exercise 2 Thought Question

There is a pattern in the answers to Exercise 1 that shows the effects debits and credits have on assets and obligations. See if you can identify it by filling in all the spaces in the following matrix with either the word <u>increase</u> or <u>decrease</u>.

Effects of:

	Debits	Credits
Cash		
Receivables		
Goods		
Payables		
Owners' Equity		

Assets — Cash, Receivables, Goods

Obligations — Payables, Owners' Equity

Exercise 2 Solution

		Effects of:	
		Debits	Credits
Assets	Cash	Increase	Decrease
	Receivables	Increase	Decrease
	Goods	Increase	Decrease
Obligations	Payables	Decrease	Increase
	Owners' Equity	Decrease	Increase

What the above solution essentially illustrates is known as the Balance Sheet Equation and its rules of debit and credit. It is shown as:

Assets	=	Liabilities (i.e., Payables)	+	Owners' Equity
Debits Credits		Debits Credits		Debits Credits
Increase+ Decrease-		Decrease- Increase+		Decrease- Increase+

Chapter Two
Accounts and Recording

In this chapter, a comprehensive example of accounting for a repair service business entity, the APEX Corporation, is begun. The example will be continued in Chapter Three and concluded in Chapter Four.

Journal and Ledger

The first step in the accounting process is to make journal entries in the Journal, the first book of accounting entry. In making the journal entries for the APEX Corp., the following categories called accounts will be debited or credited:

1.	Assets	Cash, Receivables (Claims) and Goods(Unexpired Embodied Costs)
2.	Liabilities	Payables (Obligations to non-owners)
3.	Owners' Equity	Capital Stock[1] (Obligation to owners for their investments) Retained Earnings (Obligation to owners for undistributed assets earned through operations.)
4.	Revenues	Goods or Services Given (Embodied Revenue)
5.	Expenses	Goods or Services Received which have expired (Expired Embodied Costs)

In the exchange journal entries which follow, the item received will be indicated after the account debited, and the item given after the account credited. For reclassification entries, the account from which the previously recorded data is transferred and the account to which the data is transferred will be identified. Furthermore, each account debited and credited will be identified as being either an Asset (A), Liability (L), Owners' Equity (OE), Revenue (R), or Expense (E) account, and the effect (+ or -) of the debit or credit on that account will be indicated. (In actual practice, the journal entries would not include this additional information.)

After each journal entry is made in the Journal, the debit and credit amounts will be transferred ("posted") to the Ledger, the second book of accounting entry. In posting the journal entry to the ledger accounts, the journal entry number will be included to provide a cross-reference to the Journal. The effect (+ or -) of a debit or a credit to a ledger account will be indicated at the top of each account. As each journal entry is posted, the information shown in the ledger will accumulate until after the last entry is made. At that point, the financial statements of

---

[1] There are different types of capital stock with varying legal characteristics that can be issued by a corporation. For our purpose one generic Capital Stock account will be used.

21

the company will be prepared from the information contained in the ledger accounts. The entire process can be depicted as follows:

We will now proceed by making the journal entries in the Journal and immediately posting them to the Ledger. The Ledger will be reproduced after each posting to show the cumulative data to date.

APEX Corp.
Journal

(1)   Description: On Jan. 1 2001, owners invest $100,000 in the APEX Corp. to establish it; capital stock is issued to them as evidence of ownership.

            Analysis: This is an exchange; the company <u>received</u> cash from owners and <u>gave</u> an obligation to them for their investment.

            Journal Entry (1): Dr: Cash (received) (+A) $100,000
                                 Cr: Capital Stock $100,000
                                 (obligation to owners given) (+OE)

APEX Corp.
Ledger

Assets (Resources)

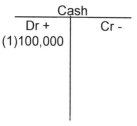

Cash

Dr +	Cr -
(1)100,000	

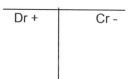

Dr +	Cr -

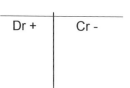

Dr +	Cr -

Dr +	Cr -

Liabilities (Obligations)

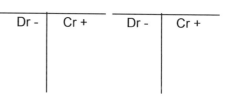

Dr -	Cr +	Dr -	Cr +

Owners' Equity (Obligations)

Capital Stock

Dr -	Cr +
	(1)100,000

Retained Earnings

Dr-	Cr+

Revenue (Goods and Services Given)

Dr -	Cr +

Expenses (Goods and Services Received used this year)

Dr +	Cr -	Dr +	Cr -

Dr +	Cr -

Income Summary

Dr	Cr

APEX Corp.
Journal

(2)   Description: A small storage building is purchased for $60,000 cash.

Analysis: This is an exchange; the company <u>received</u> a building (unexpired embodied cost) and <u>gave</u> cash (displacement cost).

Journal Entry(2):   Dr: Building (good received)(+A) $60,000
                     Cr: Cash (given)(-A) $60,000

APEX Corp.
Ledger

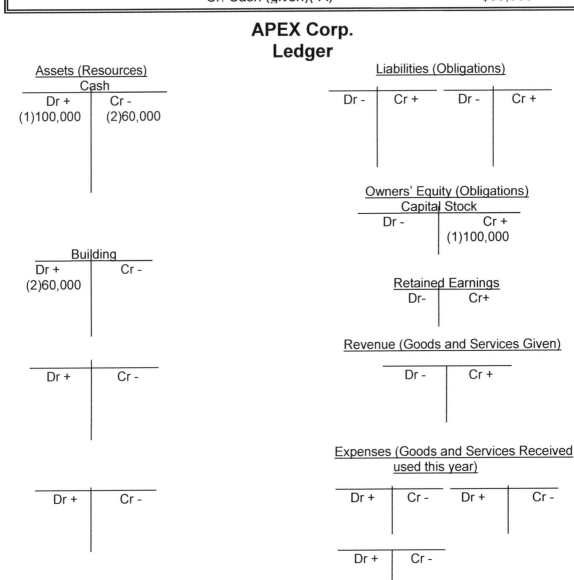

Assets (Resources)				Liabilities (Obligations)			
Cash							
Dr +	Cr -			Dr -	Cr +	Dr -	Cr +
(1)100,000	(2)60,000						

Owners' Equity (Obligations)
Capital Stock

Dr -	Cr +
	(1)100,000

Building

Dr +	Cr -
(2)60,000	

Retained Earnings

Dr-	Cr+

Revenue (Goods and Services Given)

Dr -	Cr +

Dr +	Cr -

Expenses (Goods and Services Received used this year)

Dr +	Cr -	Dr +	Cr -

Dr +	Cr -

Dr +	Cr -

Income Summary

Dr	Cr

24

APEX Corp.
Journal

(3) Description: Supplies for future use are purchased on credit in the amount of $30,000.

Analysis: This is an exchange; the company <u>received</u> supplies (unexpired embodied cost) and <u>gave</u> an obligation to the seller (displacement cost).

Journal Entry(3): Dr: Supplies (goods received)(+A) $30,000
Cr: Accounts Payable $30,000
(obligation given to seller) (+L)

APEX Corp.
Ledger

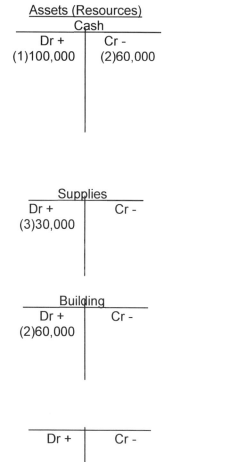

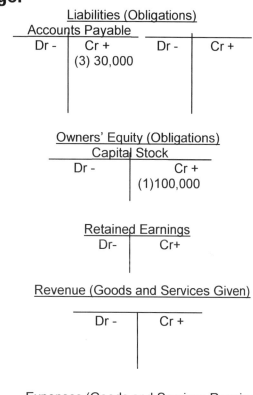

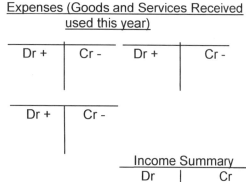

Assets (Resources)

Cash

Dr +	Cr -
(1)100,000	(2)60,000

Supplies

Dr +	Cr -
(3)30,000	

Building

Dr +	Cr -
(2)60,000	

Dr +	Cr -

Liabilities (Obligations)

Accounts Payable

Dr -	Cr +	Dr -	Cr +
	(3) 30,000		

Owners' Equity (Obligations)

Capital Stock

Dr -	Cr +
	(1)100,000

Retained Earnings

Dr-	Cr+

Revenue (Goods and Services Given)

Dr -	Cr +

Expenses (Goods and Services Received used this year)

Dr +	Cr -	Dr +	Cr -

Dr +	Cr -

Income Summary

Dr	Cr

25

APEX Corp.
Journal

(4)   Description: A $20,000 payment is made to the seller for 2/3 of the supplies purchased on credit in (3).

         Analysis: This is an exchange; the company gave cash and received a release from its obligation to the seller.

         Journal Entry(4):   Dr: Accounts Payable (release from $20,000
                            obligation to seller received) (-L)
                        Cr: Cash (given) (-A) $20,000

APEX Corp.
Ledger

Assets (Resources)

Cash

Dr +	Cr -
(1)100,000	(2) 60,000
	(4) 20,000

Supplies

Dr +	Cr -
(3)30,000	

Building

Dr +	Cr -
(2)60,000	

Dr +	Cr -

Liabilities (Obligations)

Accounts Payable

Dr -	Cr +
(4) 20,000	(3) 30,000

Dr -	Cr +

Owners' Equity (Obligations)

Capital Stock

Dr -	Cr +
	(1)100,000

Retained Earnings

Dr-	Cr+

Revenue (Goods and Services Given)

Dr -	Cr +

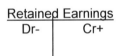

Expenses (Goods and Services Received used this year)

Dr +	Cr -	Dr +	Cr -

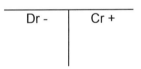

Dr +	Cr -

Income Summary

Dr	Cr

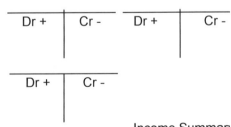

APEX Corp.
Journal

(5) Description: Repair service is performed for customers on credit at a billed price of $64,000.

Analysis: This is an exchange; the company <u>gave</u> service to customers (embodied revenue) and <u>received</u> a claim against the customers (acquisition revenue).

Journal Entry(5): Dr: Accounts Receivable (claim against $64,000
                         customers received) (+A)
                    Cr: Service Revenue (services given) (+R) $64.000

APEX Corp.
Ledger

Assets (Resources)

Cash

Dr +	Cr -
(1)100,000	(2) 60,000
	(4) 20,000

Accounts Receivable

Dr +	Cr -
(5)64,000	

Supplies

Dr +	Cr -
(3)30,000	

Building

Dr +	Cr -
(2)60,000	

Liabilities (Obligations)

Accounts Payable

Dr -	Cr +	Dr -	Cr +
(4) 20,000	(3) 30,000		

Owners' Equity (Obligations)

Capital Stock

Dr -	Cr +
	(1)100,000

Retained Earnings

Dr-	Cr+

Revenue (Goods and Services Given)

Service Revenue

Dr -	Cr +
	(5) 64,000

Expenses (Goods and Services Received used this year)

Dr +	Cr -	Dr +	Cr -

Dr +	Cr -

Income Summary

Dr	Cr

27

APEX Corp.
Journal

(6)   Description: Customers remit $40,000 in partial payment of the accounts receivable recorded in (5).

Analysis: This is an exchange; the company <u>received</u> cash and <u>gave</u> customers a release from its claim against them.

Journal Entry(6):   Dr: Cash (received) (+A) $40,000
    Cr: Accounts Receivable $40,000
    (release given to customers
    from claim against them) (-A)

APEX Corp.
Ledger

Assets (Resources)

Cash

Dr +	Cr -
(1)100,000	(2) 60,000
(6)40,000	(4) 20,000

Accounts Receivable

Dr +	Cr -
(5)64,000	(6)40,000

Supplies

Dr +	Cr -
(3)30,000	

Building

Dr +	Cr -
(2)60,000	

Liabilities (Obligations)

Accounts Payable

Dr -	Cr +	Dr -	Cr +
(4) 20,000	(3) 30,000		

Owners' Equity (Obligations)

Capital Stock

Dr -	Cr +
	(1)100,000

Retained Earnings

Dr-	Cr+

Revenue (Goods and Services Given)

Service Revenue

Dr -	Cr +
	(5) 64,000

Expenses (Goods and Services Received used this year)

Dr +	Cr -	Dr +	Cr -

Dr +	Cr -

Income Summary

Dr	Cr

APEX Corp.
Journal

(7) Description: Salaries of $16,000 are owed to employees for services performed; payment will be made later.

Analysis: This is an exchange; the company received employee services (expired embodied cost) and gave an obligation to employees (displacement cost).

Journal Entry(7): Dr: Salary Expense $16,000
        (employee services received) (+E)
        Cr: Salaries Payable $16,000
        (obligation to employees given) (+L)

APEX Corp.
Ledger

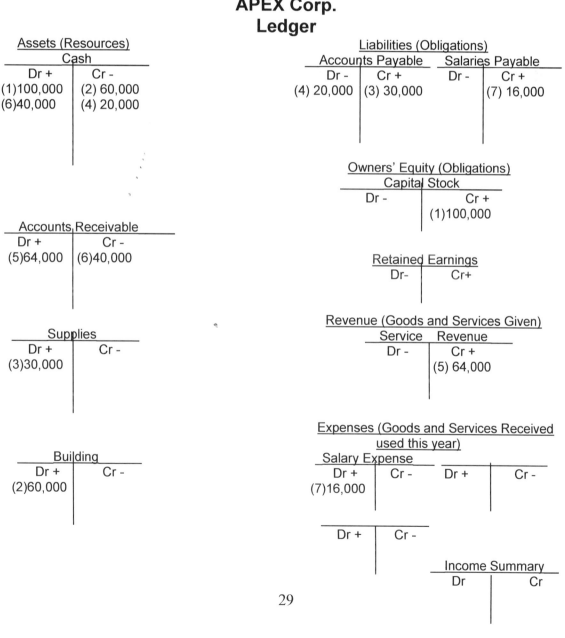

Assets (Resources)

Cash
Dr +	Cr -
(1)100,000	(2) 60,000
(6)40,000	(4) 20,000

Accounts Receivable
Dr +	Cr -
(5)64,000	(6)40,000

Supplies
Dr +	Cr -
(3)30,000	

Building
Dr +	Cr -
(2)60,000	

Liabilities (Obligations)

Accounts Payable
Dr -	Cr +
(4) 20,000	(3) 30,000

Salaries Payable
Dr -	Cr +
	(7) 16,000

Owners' Equity (Obligations)

Capital Stock
Dr -	Cr +
	(1)100,000

Retained Earnings
Dr-	Cr+

Revenue (Goods and Services Given)

Service Revenue
Dr -	Cr +
	(5) 64,000

Expenses (Goods and Services Received used this year)

Salary Expense
Dr +	Cr -
(7)16,000	

Dr +	Cr -

Dr +	Cr -

Income Summary
Dr	Cr

29

APEX Corp.
Journal

(8) Description: $22,000 of the previously purchased supplies were used during the period.

Analysis: A reclassification entry is needed to transfer $22,000 <u>from</u> the Supplies Asset (unexpired cost) <u>to</u> Supplies Expense (expired cost).

Journal Entry(8): Dr: Supplies Expense (to) (+E) $22,000
                        Cr: Supplies (from) (-A) $22,000

APEX Corp.
Ledger

Assets (Resources)

Cash

Dr +	Cr -
(1)100,000	(2) 60,000
(6)40,000	(4) 20,000

Accounts Receivable

Dr +	Cr -
(5)64,000	(6)40,000

Supplies

Dr +	Cr -
(3)30,000	(8)22,000

Building

Dr +	Cr -
(2)60,000	

Liabilities (Obligations)

Accounts Payable

Dr -	Cr +
(4) 20,000	(3) 30,000

Salaries Payable

Dr -	Cr +
	(7) 16,000

Owners' Equity (Obligations)

Capital Stock

Dr -	Cr +
	(1)100,000

Retained Earnings

Dr-	Cr+

Revenue (Goods and Services Given)

Service Revenue

Dr -	Cr +
	(5) 64,000

Expenses (Goods and Services Received used this year)

Salary Expense

Dr +	Cr -
(7)16,000	

Supplies Expense

Dr +	Cr -
(8)22,000	

Dr +	Cr -

Income Summary

Dr	Cr

APEX Corp.
Journal

(9)   Description: At the end of the year, the building is estimated to have exhausted 1 year of its expected 10 year life, i.e., it has depreciated by 10%.

           Analysis: A reclassification entry is needed to transfer $6,000 (10% of the $60,000 building cost) from the Building Asset (unexpired cost) to Depreciation Expense (expired cost).

           Journal Entry(9):   Dr: Depreciation Expense (to) (+E) $6,000
                           Cr: Building (from)* (-A) $6,000

*There is an alternative way to record this entry, which uses an Accumulated Depreciation account; it is covered in Chapter Six.

APEX Corp.
Ledger

Assets (Resources)

Cash

Dr +	Cr -
(1)100,000	(2) 60,000
(6)40,000	(4) 20,000

Accounts Receivable

Dr +	Cr -
(5)64,000	(6)40,000

Supplies

Dr +	Cr -
(3)30,000	(8)22,000

Building

Dr +	Cr -
(2)60,000	(9)6,000

Liabilities (Obligations)

Accounts Payable		Salaries Payable	
Dr -	Cr +	Dr -	Cr +
(4) 20,000	(3) 30,000		(7) 16,000

Owners' Equity (Obligations)

Capital Stock

Dr -	Cr +
	(1)100,000

Retained Earnings

Dr-	Cr+

Revenue (Goods and Services Given)

Service Revenue

Dr -	Cr +
	(5) 64,000

Expenses (Goods and Services Received used this year)

Salary Expense		Supplies Expense	
Dr +	Cr -	Dr +	Cr -
(7)16,000		(8)22,000	

Depreciation Expense

Dr +	Cr -
(9)6,000	

Income Summary

Dr	Cr

31

At this point summations of the debit and credit amounts in each account will be made and the difference between the two, the <u>account balance (Bal.)</u> will be found for each account.

APEX Corp.
Ledger

Assets (Resources)

Cash

Dr +	Cr -
(1)100,000	(2) 60,000
(6)40,000	(4) 20,000
140,000	80,000

Bal.   60,000

Accounts Receivable

Dr +	Cr -
(5)64,000	(6)40,000

Bal. 24,000

Supplies

Dr +	Cr -
(3)30,000	(8)22,000

Bal. 8,000

Building

Dr +	Cr -
(2)60,000	(9)6,000

Bal. 54,000

Liabilities (Obligations)

Accounts Payable		Salaries Payable	
Dr -	Cr +	Dr -	Cr +
(4) 20,000	(3) 30,000		(7) 16,000 Bal.
	10,000 Bal.		

Owners' Equity (Obligations)

Capital Stock

Dr -	Cr +
	(1)100,000 Bal.

Retained Earnings

Dr-	Cr+

Revenue (Goods and Services Given)

Service   Revenue

Dr -	Cr +
	(5) 64,000 Bal.

Expenses (Goods and Services Received used this year)

Salary Expense		Supplies Expense	
Dr +	Cr -	Dr +	Cr -
Bal.(7)16,000		Bal.(8)22,000	

Depreciation Expense

Dr +	Cr -
Bal.(9)6,000	

Income Summary

Dr	Cr

We will now go to Chapter Three and prepare financial statements from the account balances above. But, before proceeding, do the exercises that follow. Solutions are provided.

Exercise 1 Journal Entries and Accounts

A list of accounts follows:

>   Cash
>   Accounts Receivable
>   Supplies
>   Truck
>   Note Payable
>   Utilities Payable
>   Service Revenue
>   Depreciation Expense
>   Interest Expense
>   Salaries Expense
>   Supplies Expense
>   Utilities Expense

For each numbered statement below, make the journal entry (without amounts) to record the exchange or the required reclassification. Select the accounts to be used from the list given above. After each account debited and credited, indicate whether the account is an Asset (A), Liability (L),Revenue (R), or Expense (E) account and whether the account would be increased (+) or decreased (-) by the debit or credit.

Example: Cash is received from customers for services given to them.

>   Dr: Cash(+A)
>   Cr: Service Revenue (+R)

1. Cash is received from a bank and an obligation in the form of a note is given.

2. A truck is purchased for cash.

3. Supplies for later use are purchased for cash.

4. Employee services are received and cash is paid to them.

5. A claim against a customer is received for services given.

6. Part of the supplies purchased in 3 above were used in providing the services in 5 above.

7. Cash is received from the customer in 5 above and a release from the claim is given

8. Interest (use of money service received) is recorded on the note signed in 1 above and cash is given to the bank.

9. A release from the note obligation to the bank is received in return for cash given to liquidate it.

10. Utility services are received and an obligation to pay later is given.

11. A release from the utility obligation in 10 above is received in return for cash paid.

12. Depreciation for the year on the truck is recorded.

Exercise 1 Solution:

1. Dr: Cash (+A)
   Cr: Note Payable (+L)

2. Dr: Truck (+A)
   Cr: Cash (-A)

3. Dr: Supplies (+A)
   Cr: Cash (-A)

4. Dr: Salaries Expense (+E)
   Cr: Cash (-A)

5. Dr: Accounts Receivable (+A)
   Cr: Service Revenue (+R)

6. Dr: Supplies Expense (+E)
   Cr: Supplies (-A)
   (This is a reclassification)

7. Dr: Cash (+A)
   Cr: Accounts Receivable (-A)

8. Dr: Interest Expense (+E)
   Cr: Cash (-A)

9. Dr: Note Payable (-L)
   Cr: Cash (-A)

10. Dr: Utilities Expense (+E)
    Cr: Utilities Payable (+L)

11. Dr: Utilities Payable (-L)
    Cr: Cash (-A)

12. Dr: Depreciation Expense(+E)
    Cr: Truck(-A)
    (This is a reclassification)

Exercise 2 Account Balances

Assuming a balance is reached for each of the following ledger accounts, indicate by an X whether it would normally be a debit or credit balance.

Account   Type of Balance

	Debit	Credit
Example: Cash (Asset)	X	
1. Revenue		
2. Expense		
3. Receivable (Asset)		
4. Unexpired Goods (Asset)		
5. Payable (Liability)		
6. Capital Stock (Owners' Equity)		

Exercise 2 Solution

Account   Type of Balance

	Debit	Credit
Example: Cash (Asset)	X	
2. Revenue		X
3. Expense	X	
4. Receivable (Asset)	X	
5. Unexpired Goods (Asset)	X	
6. Payable (Liability)		X
7. Capital Stock (Owners' Equity)		X

Chapter Three
Financial Statements

This chapter continues the APEX Corp. example begun in Chapter Two. Financial statements will be prepared and discussed and the year-end closing process illustrated. The interaction (articulation) of the financial statements is also covered along with the effects of journal entries on the statements.

Financial Statements

The information for the preparation of the financial statements of the APEX Corp. comes from the ledger accounts shown at the end of Chapter Two. For reference, these ledger accounts are reproduced below.

APEX Corp.
Ledger

Assets (Resources)

Cash

Dr +	Cr -
(1)100,000	(2) 60,000
(6)40,000	(4) 20,000
140,000	80,000
Bal. 60,000	

Accounts Receivable

Dr +	Cr -
(5)64,000	(6)40,000
Bal. 24,000	

Supplies

Dr +	Cr -
(3)30,000	(8)22,000
Bal. 8,000	

Building

Dr +	Cr -
(2)60,000	(9)6,000
Bal. 54,000	

Liabilities (Obligations)

Accounts Payable

Dr -	Cr +
(4) 20,000	(3) 30,000
	10,000 Bal.

Salaries Payable

Dr -	Cr +
	(7) 16,000 Bal.

Owners' Equity (Obligations)

Capital Stock

Dr -	Cr +
	(1)100,000 Bal.

Retained Earnings

Dr-	Cr+

Revenue (Goods and Services Given)

Service Revenue

Dr -	Cr +
	(5) 64,000 Bal.

Expenses (Goods and Services Received used this year)

Salary Expense

Dr +	Cr -
Bal.(7)16,000	

Supplies Expense

Dr +	Cr -
Bal.(8)22,000	

Depreciation Expense

Dr +	Cr -
Bal.(9)6,000	

Income Summary

Dr	Cr

Before preparing the financial statements, it is useful to prepare a trial balance to check the equality of the debit and credit balances in the ledger. The trial balance is simply a listing and summation of these balances. The APEX Corp. trial balance is shown below.

APEX Corp.
Trial Balance
Dec. 31, 2001

Debit Balances		Credit Balances	
Cash	$60,000	Accounts Payable	$10,000
Accounts Receivable	24,000	Salaries Payable	16,000
Supplies	8,000	Capital Stock	100,000
Building	54,000	Service Revenue	64,000
Salary Expense	16,000		
Supplies Expense	22,000		
Depreciation Expense	6,000		
Total	$190,000	Total	$190,000

The balances from the trial balance (or from the ledger accounts themselves) are now used for the preparation of the financial statements. The APEX Corp. statements which will be prepared are the Income Statement, the Statement of Retained Earnings, and the Balance Sheet.[1]

APEX Corp.
Income Statement
For the Year Ended Dec. 31, 2001

Service Revenue		$64,000
Expenses:		
Supplies Expense	$22,000	
Salary Expense	$16,000	
Depreciation Expense	$6,000	
		-44,000
Net Income		$20,000

In the Income Statement, Revenue shows the amount and type of goods and service given sold) to customers during the period. And equally important, Revenue reflects the increase in net assets received from the sale of those goods and services. To elaborate, net assets is the difference between assets held and liabilities owed. That is:

Total Assets
-Total Liabilities
=Net Assets

Another financial statement, the Cash Flow Statement will be covered in Chapter Four.

To understand how revenue entries increase net assets, think back to the APEX Corp. journal entry that <u>credited</u> service revenue. In that entry, the <u>debit</u> increased an accounts receivable asset which <u>increased net assets by $64,000</u>.

<u>Expenses</u> in the Income Statement show the amount and type of <u>goods and services received</u> (purchased) that were used up during the current period. But also, <u>Expenses</u> reflect <u>decreases in net assets</u>. To understand how expense entries decrease net assets, recall the APEX Corp. journal entries that <u>debited</u> building depreciation expense and supplies expense. In those entries, the <u>credits</u> decreased the building and supplies assets which <u>decreased net assets by $6,000 and $22,000</u> respectively. And, in the APEX Corp. entry <u>debiting</u> salary expense, the <u>credit</u> increased a salaries payable liability which <u>decreased net assets by $16,000</u>. The overall impact of all the aforementioned revenue and expense entries was a <u>$20,000 increase in the net assets</u> earned from operations.

Based on the foregoing discussion, the following comprehensive definitions of revenue, expense and net income can be developed using the two senses of revenue and cost.

Revenue: the increase in net assets (acquisition revenue) resulting from goods and services given (embodied revenue).

-Expense: the decrease in net assets (displacement cost) resulting from goods and services received and used (embodied cost).

=Net Income: the overall increase in net assets from operations earned for owners for their services (e.g., investing and perhaps personal services). [XI]

The next financial statement is the Statement of Retained Earnings. Retained Earnings is an owners' equity account, and it shows the corporation's obligation to its owners for earned net assets (i.e., net income) not yet distributed to them. The Statement of Retained Earnings is shown below with explanatory parenthetical comments included.

40

APEX Corp.
Statement of Retained Earnings
For the Year Ended Dec. 31, 2001

Retained Earnings, Jan. 1, 2001 (obligation to owners for undistributed earned net assets at the beginning of the year.)	$0
Net Income (increase in obligation to owners for the year's earned net assets)	20,000
Retained Earnings, Dec. 31, 2001 (obligation to owners for undistributed earned net assets at the end of the year.)	$20,000

Before going on, be sure to note how the net income figure was carried forward from the Income Statement to the Statement of Retained Earnings to show the increase in the Retained Earnings obligation to owners for net assets earned this year. (This increase in Retained Earnings will be recorded in the ledger accounts in the closing process discussed in the next section.)

The Balance Sheet[2] follows. In it, note especially the carrying forward of the final Retained Earnings figure from the Statement of Retained Earnings to the Balance Sheet. This incorporates into the Balance Sheet the entity's obligation to owners for the earned net assets. This causes the Balance Sheet to balance since inclusion of the Retained Earnings obligation on the right side of the Balance Sheet counterbalances the earned net assets included in the total assets figure on the left side.

This is the commonly used name for this statement. In a formal presentation it would be labeled The Statement of Financial Condition.

APEX Corp.
Balance Sheet
At Dec. 31, 2001

Assets (Resources)		Liabilities and Owners' Equity (Obligations)	
Cash	$60,000	Liabilities:(Obligations to non-owners)	
Accounts Receivable (Claims)	24,000		
Supplies (Unexpired Cost)	8,000	Accounts Payable	$10,000
Building (Unexpired Cost)	54,000	Salaries Payable	$16,000
			$26,000
		Owners' Equity:	
		Capital Stock (Obligation to owners for investment)	$100,000
		Retained Earnings (Obligation to owners for undistributed earned net assets)	$20,000
			$120,000
Total Assets	$146,000 =	Total Liabilities and Owner's Equity	$146,000

The Balance Sheet shows the total assets (resources) held by the company at the end of the year and the total obligations it owes at the end of the year. The total assets are equal to the total obligations because all of the assets held by the company are owed to someone, either non-owners or owners. Before we leave the Balance Sheet, let's look again at the idea of net assets. The net assets of the APEX Corp. contained in the Balance Sheet at year-end are:

Assets	$146,000
-Liabilities	−26,000
Net Assets	$120,000 = Owners' Equity of $120,000

Note that the net assets equal the total owners' equity obligation to the owners at year-end. In other words, if the liabilities were paid off, the remaining assets would be owed to the owners. Or to put it another way, the owners have a residual claim, after liabilities, against the assets of the company.

Closing Entries

Closing journal entries are made and posted to the ledger at the end of the year for purposes of bringing the revenue and expense accounts to zero balances, recording net income (or loss), and updating retained earnings. The information for the closing entries comes from the revenue and expense balances shown in the ledger accounts at the beginning of this chapter.

Three closing entries will now be made and posted to the ledger accounts. The first closing entry (C_1) is a reclassification entry which closes out the revenue account by transferring its credit balance to an Income Summary account. The entry is:

(C_1) **Dr: Service Revenue**   **$64,000 (From)**
         Cr: Income Summary   **$64,000 (To)**

The second closing entry (C_2) is also a reclassification entry which closes out the expense accounts by transferring the total of their debit balances to the Income Summary account. This entry, in what is called compound form is:

(C_2) **Dr: Income Summary**   **$44,000(To)**
         Cr: Supplies Expense   **$22,000(From)**
         Cr: Salary Expense   **$16,000(From)**
         Cr: Depreciation   **$6,000(From)**
         Expense

The third closing entry (C_3) is actually an exchange entry between the company and the owners in which the debit records the amount of the net income as indicative of the value of owner services received.[XII] The credit records the retained earnings obligation given to owners for this year's earned net assets. The entry is:

(C_3) **Dr: Income Summary** (for net   **$20,000**
       income reflecting a positive
       value for owner services
       received equal to earned net assets)[3]
         Cr: Retained Earnings   **$20,000**
         (obligation given to owners
         for earned net assets.)

---

[3] When a company has a net loss for the period the closing entries would be as follows (figures are assumed):

Journal Entry (C_1) **Dr: Revenue**   **$80,000 (from)**
         Cr: Income Summary   **$80,000 (to)**
Journal Entry (C_2) **Dr: Income Summary**   **$90,000 (to)**
         Cr: Expenses   **$90,000 (from)**
Journal Entry (C_3) **Dr: Retained Earnings**   **$10,000**
       (release received from obligation to
       owner because of net assets lost)
       Cr: Income Summary   **$10,000**
       (for net loss reflecting a negative
        value for owner services received
        equal to net assets lost)

43

The three closing entries will now be posted to the ledger accounts. After these postings, the accounts would appear as follows:

APEX Corp.
Ledger

Assets (Resources)

Cash

Dr +	Cr -
(1)100,000	(2) 60,000
(6)40,000	(4) 20,000
140,000	80,000
Bal. 60,000	

Accounts Receivable

Dr +	Cr -
(5)64,000	(6)40,000
Bal. 24,000	

Supplies

Dr +	Cr -
(3)30,000	(8)22,000
Bal. 8,000	

Building

Dr +	Cr -
(2)60,000	(9)6,000
Bal. 54,000	

Liabilities (Obligations)

Accounts Payable		Salaries Payable	
Dr -	Cr +	Dr -	Cr +
(4) 20,000	(3) 30,000		(7) 16,000 Bal.
	10,000 Bal.		

Owners' Equity (Obligations)

Capital Stock

Dr -	Cr +
	(1)100,000 Bal.

Retained Earnings

	(C$_3$) 20,000 Bal.

Revenue (Goods and Services Given)

Service Revenue

Dr -	Cr +
(C$_1$)64,000	(5) 64,000 Bal.

Expenses (Goods and Services Received used this year)

Salary Expense		Supplies Expense	
Dr +	Cr -	Dr +	Cr -
Bal.(7)16,000	(C$_2$)16,000	Bal.(8)22,000	(C$_2$)22,000

Depreciation Expense: Building

Dr +	Cr -
Bal.(9)6,000	(C$_2$) 6,000

Income Summary

Dr	Cr
expenses (C$_2$) 44,000	(C$_1$)64,000
net income (C$_3$) 20,000	
64,000	64,000

In the foregoing ledger accounts, note that net income has been recorded and retained earnings now has a balance. Also, the revenue, expense, and income summary accounts have no balances i.e., they have been "closed out" so as to prepare them for the recording of next year's revenue and expense data. The assets, liabilities, and owners' equity accounts "stay open" and show the balances with which the company will begin the next year.

Journal Entry Effects

Since journal entries provide the raw data which ultimately appears in the income statement and balance sheet, it is important at the time of making an entry to be aware of the effect the entry will have on those statements. The effects of debits and credits to asset, liability and owners' equity accounts are straightforward in that they only affect the balance sheet. These balance sheet effects, as seen previously are:

	Debit	**Credit**
Assets	+Increases	-Decreases
Liabilities	-Decreases	+Increases
Owners' Equity	-Decreases	+Increases

The effects of revenue credits and expense debits, on the other hand, are more complex since they affect both the income statement and the balance sheet. As an aid in understanding the financial statement effects of revenue and expense entries, Illustration I below summarizes the previously discussed interaction (articulation) of the APEX Corp. financial statements.

Illustration I
Financial Statement Interaction
APEX Corp.

Income Statement	Statement of Retained Earnings	Balance Sheet
Revenue $64,000	Beg. Retained	Assets $146,000 Liabilities $26,000
-Expenses-44,000	Earnings $0	
Net Inc. $20,000 ──► Net Income 20,000		Owners' Equity:
	End. Retained	Capital Stock 100,000
	Earnings $20,000 ──►	Retained Earnings 20,000
		Liabilities+
	Assets $146,000 Owners' Equity $146,000	

Illustration I shows that Revenue (R) has a positive effect on Net Income (NI) in the Income Statement (I/S) which in turn has a positive effect on Retained Earnings (RE) and therefore total Owners' Equity (OE) in the Balance Sheet (B/S). Therefore, a journal entry credit to Revenue has the following financial statement effects:

Dr: Other account
Cr: Revenue (+R+NI in I/S,+RE+OE in B/S)

Illustration I also shows that Expenses (E) have a negative effect on Net Income (NI) in the Income Statement (I/S) which in turn has a negative effect on Retained Earnings (RE) and Owners' Equity (OE) in the Balance Sheet (B/S). Therefore a journal entry <u>debit to Expense</u> has the following financial statement effects:

Dr: Expense (+E-NI in I/S,-RE-OE in B/S)
Cr: Other account

A summary of financial statement effects of journal entries is presented in Table I below.

Table I
Journal Entry Effects
On Financial Statements

	Debit	Credit
Assets	+A in B/S	-A in B/S
Liabilities	-L in B/S	+L in B/S
Owner's Equity:		
Capital Stock	-OE in B/S	+OE in B/S
Retained Earnings	-OE in B/S	+OE in B/S
Revenue	*	+R+NI in I/S, +RE+OE in B/S
Expense	+E-NI in I/S, -RE-OE in B/S	*

*Such entries are infrequent. Typically, they would be made for correction purposes and in the closing process.

The APEX Corp. example will be continued and concluded in Chapter Four. An Appendix discussing the Balance Sheet Equation follows. Then, two exercises follow.

Appendix

The Balance Sheet Equation

Table 1 presented on the preceding page shows the effects accounting entries have on a company's financial statements. Another way to show these effects is through use of the balance sheet equation which is:

$$\underline{\text{Assets}} \quad = \quad \underline{\text{Liabilities}} \quad + \quad \underline{\text{Owners' Equity}}$$

Assets			Liabilities			Owners' Equity	
Dr.	Cr.		Dr.	Cr.		Dr.	Cr.
+	−		−	+		−	+

Expense   Revenue
Dr. −NI   Cr. +NI

Note that the + and − effects shown in the above equation can be used as rules for recording debit/credit entries. For example: increases in assets are recorded by debits and decreases by credits. The opposite is true for liabilities and owners' equity with increases recorded by credits and decreases by debits. Expenses and revenues are treated as negative and positive sub-categories of owners' equity with expenses recorded by debits and revenues by credits.

Very often the above rules serve as the basis for introductory accounting instruction. This tends to lead to memorization on the part of students and as a result they apply the rules without an awareness of why they exist and the logic behind them. One of purposes of this book is to have readers understand that the financial statement effects (i.e., balance sheet equation rules) result from the recording of exchanges by debiting what is received and crediting what is concurrently given. Using this received/given logic, the balance sheet effects resulting from debit (received) entries (i.e., +A, − L, − OE) and from credit (given) entries (i.e., − A , +L, +OE) become readily apparent. Similarly, the reclassification of previously recorded exchange data from one account to another clearly shows the resultant balance sheet effects (i.e., rules).

It is hoped that students using the balance sheet equation approach will (1) expand their thought process when recording exchanges so as to include identification of what is received and what is given and, (2) become cognizant of the results of the "from -> to" process of exchange reclassification. By doing this, the student will understand why the balance sheet effects exist and the logic underlying them. This will add a conceptual component to his or her memorization-based thought process which will make accounting more understandable, meaningful, and palatable.

Exercise 1 Financial Statement Preparation and Closing Entries

An alphabetical listing of accounts and their ledger balances is given below.

Accounts and Balances (in 000's)

Accounts Payable	$ 8
Accounts Receivable	20
Capital Stock	78
Cash	85
Depreciation Expense	9
Equipment	81
Interest Expense	4
Interest Payable	4
Note Payable	60
Retained Earnings (beginning balance)	0
Salary Expense	32
Service Revenue	129
Supplies	19
Supplies Expense	17
Utilities Expense	12

Instructions: Using the above data, prepare an Income Statement, Statement of Retained Earnings and a Balance Sheet. Then prepare closing entries.

Exercise 1 Solution

Income Statement

Service Revenue		$129
Expenses:		
Salary Expense	$32	
Supplies Expense	17	
Utilities Expense	12	
Depreciation Expense	9	
Interest Expense	4	
Total Expenses		-74
Net Income		$55

Statement of Retained Earnings

Retained Earnings (beginning of year)	$ 0
Net Income	+55
Retained Earnings (end of year)	$55

Balance Sheet

Assets		Liabilities and Owner's Equity	
Cash	$85	Liabilities:	
Accounts Receivable	20	Accounts Payable	$ 8
Supplies	19	Note Payable	60
Equipment	81	Interest Payable	4
			$72
		Owner's Equity:	
		Capital Stock	$78
		Retained Earnings	55
			$133
Total Assets	$205	Total Liabilities and Owner's Equity	$205

Closing Entries

1. Dr: Service Revenue $129
       Cr: Income Summary $129

2. Dr: Income Summary $74
       Cr: Salary Expense $32
       Cr: Supplies Expense   17
       Cr: Utilities Expense   12
       Cr: Depreciation Expense   9
       Cr: Interest Expense   4

3. Dr: Income Summary $55
       Cr: Retained Earnings $55

Exercise 2 Effects of Journal Entries

Make journal entries, without amounts, for each of the numbered items given below. After each account debited and credited indicate its effect (+ or -) on the following six components of the financial statements. Use the following code:

Revenue	(R)	**Assets**	(A)
Expense	(E)	**Liabilities**	(L)
Net Income	(NI)	**Owners' Equity**	(OE)
		(which includes both	
		Capital Stock and	
		Retained Earnings)	

Example: Cash was received for services given to customers.

> **Dr: Cash (+A)**
> **Cr: Service Revenue (+R+NI+OE)**

1. Services were given to customers on credit.

2. The customers in 1 remitted cash.

3. Supplies were purchased on credit.

4. Payment was made for the supplies purchased in 3.

5. Some of the supplies were used.

51

6. Equipment was purchased for a note payable given.

7. Depreciation on the equipment was recorded.

8. Electricity service was received and recorded as utilities payable owed.

9. Employee services were received and cash paid

10. Additional capital stock was issued to owners in return for cash received.

Exercise 2 Solution

1. Dr: Accounts Receivable (+A)
      Cr: Service Revenue (+R+NI+OE)

2. Dr: Cash (+A)
      Cr: Accounts Receivable (-A)

3. Dr: Supplies (+A)
      Cr: Accounts Payable (+L)

4. Dr: Accounts Payable (-L)
      Cr: Cash (-A)

5. Dr: Supplies Expense (+E-NI-OE)
      Cr: Supplies (-A)

6. Dr: Equipment (+A)
      Cr: Note Payable (+L)

7. Dr: Depreciation Expense (+E-NI-OE)
      Cr: Equipment (-A)

8. Dr: Electricity Expense (+E-NI-OE)
      Cr: Utilities Payable (+L)

9. Dr: Salary Expense (+E-NI-OE)
      Cr: Cash (-A)

10. Dr: Cash (+A)
      Cr: Capital Stock (+OE)

Chapter Four

Comprehensive Example

This chapter continues the APEX Corp. example for a second year, 2002. Significant additions to the preceding first-year 2001 example are:

1. The company is expanded so as to sell merchandise in addition to providing service.
2. Corporate income taxes are included
3. A dividend is paid to owners (stockholders).
4. The balance sheet is presented in classified form.
5. A cash flow statement is added.

The sequence of procedures for the second year will be:

1. Record journal entries
2. Post to ledger accounts
3. Prepare financial statements (including the cash flow statement).

Journal and Ledger

Before presenting the journal entries for 2002, the ending balances of the ledger accounts at De 31, 2001 will be shown since they become the beginning balances for the year 2002.

APEX Corp.
Ledger

Assets	Liabilities and Owners' Equity

Cash

Dr +	Cr -
12/31/01	
Bal. 60,000	

Accounts Receivable

Dr+	Cr-
12/31/01	
Bal. 24,000	

Supplies

Dr+	Cr-
12/31/01	
Bal. 8,000	

Building

Dr+	Cr-
12/31/01	
Bal.54,000	

Accounts Payable

Dr -	Cr +
	12/31/01 Bal. 10,000

Salaries Payable

Dr-	Cr+
	12/31/01 Bal. 16,000

Capital Stock

Dr -	Cr +
	12/31/01 Bal.100,000

Retained Earnings

Dr -	Cr +
	12/31/01 Bal. 20,000

The journal entries for 2002 will now be recorded. The analysis relied upon in making the entries is described parenthetically. Also, the effect (+ or -) on the financial statements of each debit and each credit is shown using the following abbreviations: Revenue R, Expense E, Net Income NI, Assets A, Liabilities L, and Owners' Equity OE.

APEX Corp.
Journal

1. The salaries payable of $16,000 from 2001 are paid (Analysis: a release from the payable obligation is received and cash is given.)

Dr: Salaries Payable (-L)	$16,000	
Cr: Cash (-A)		$16,000

2. Cash of $25,000 is borrowed from a bank and an 8% interest bearing note payable is signed. (Analysis: Cash is received and a note payable obligation is given.)

Dr: Cash (+A)	$25,000	
Cr: Notes Payable (+L)		$25,000

3. Land is purchased for a parking lot for $20,000 cash. (Analysis: Land is received and cash is given.)

Dr: Land (+A)	$20,000	
Cr: Cash (-A)		$20,000

4. Merchandise inventory for future sale is purchased on credit at a cost of $75,000. (Analysis: Inventory is received and an accounts payable obligation is given.)

Dr: Inventory[1] (+A)	$75,000	
Cr: Accounts Payable(+L)		$75,000

5. Merchandise is sold to customers on credit at a sales price of $120,000. (Analysis: An accounts receivable claim is received and goods are given which is recorded as sales revenue.)

Dr: Accounts Receivable (+A)	$120,000	
Cr: Sales Revenue (+R+NI+OE)		$120,000

---

[1] This is an illustration of the "perpetual inventory" method which debits an Inventory account at the time the goods are purchased. There is an alternate "periodic method" which debits a Purchases account. It is covered in Appendix A to this chapter.

6. The cost of the inventory sold in 5 was $65,000 and it is recorded as cost of goods sold expense. (Analysis: A reclassification entry from inventory to cost of goods sold expense is necessary to record the expiration of the inventory.)

Dr: Cost of Goods Sold Expense (+E-NI-OE) $65,000	
Cr: Inventory (-A)	**$65,000**

7. Accounts receivable of $100,000 are collected. (Analysis: Cash is received and a release from the accounts receivable claim is given.)

Dr: Cash (+A)	**$100,000**
Cr: Accounts Receivable (-A)	**$100,000**

8. Accounts payable of $65,000 are paid. (Analysis: A release from the payable obligation is received and cash is given.)

Dr: Accounts Payable (-L)	**$65,000**
Cr: Cash (-A)	**$65,000**

9. Service is provided to customers for $45,000 cash. (Analysis: Cash is received and service is given.)

Dr: Cash (+A)	**$45,000**
Cr: Service Revenue (+R+NI+OE)	**$45,000**

10. Supplies of $5,000 were used in providing the service performed in 9. (Analysis: A reclassification from supplies to supplies expense is necessary to record the expiration of the supplies.)

Dr: Supplies Expense (+E-NI-OE)	**$5,000**
Cr: Supplies (-A)	**$5,000**

11. Salaries of $25,000 are paid to employees. (Analysis: Employee service is received and cash is given.)

Dr: Salary Expense (+E-NI-OE)	**$25,000**
Cr: Cash (-A)	**$25,000**

12. Depreciation on the building for the year was $6,000. (Analysis: A reclassification from building to depreciation expense is necessary to record the expiration of the building.)

Dr: Depreciation Expense (+E-NI-OE)	**$6,000**
Cr: Building (-A)	**$6,000**

13. Interest of $2,000 (8% x $25,000) on the note payable for the year was paid. (Analysis: Use of money service was <u>received</u>, and cash is <u>given</u>.)

Dr: Interest Expense (+E-NI-OE)	$2,000	
Cr: Cash (-A)		$2,000

14. Income taxes are owed in the amount of $12,000. (Analysis: Government services were <u>received</u> and a tax payable obligation is <u>given</u>.)

Dr: Income Tax Expense (+E-NI-OE)	$12,000	
Cr: Income Tax Payable (+L)		$12,000

15. A cash dividend of $18,000 out of earned assets is paid to owners. (Analysis: A release from the retained earnings obligation is <u>received</u> and cash is <u>given</u>.)

Discussion: There are <u>two</u> ways to record the dividend.

One way would be:

Dr: Retained Earnings (-OE)	$18,000	
Cr: Cash (-A)		$18,000

The alternate way uses a Dividends account which is a negative retained earnings account. The entry is:

Dr: Dividends (-RE -OE)	$18,000	
Cr: Cash (-A)		$18,000

Later the Dividends account will be closed to retained earnings as follows:

Dr: RE	$18,000	
Cr: Dividends		$18,000

In the APEX Corp. example a Dividends account will be used.

After posting the preceding journal entries and obtaining 12/31/02 balances (except for the ending retained earnings balance which will be found after closing), the ledger accounts would appear as follows:

Ledger
Balance Sheet Accounts

Cash

Dr +	Cr -
12/31/01	
Bal. 60,000	(1) 16,000
(2)25,000	(3)20,000
(7)100,000	(8) 65,000
(9)45,000	(11)25,000
	(13)2,000
	(15)18,000
230,000	146,000
12/31/02	
Bal 84,000	

Accounts Receivable

Dr+	Cr-
12/31/01	
Bal. 24,000	
(5)120,000	(7)100,000
144,000	100,000
12/31/02	
Bal 44,000	

Inventory

Dr+	Cr-
(4)75,000	(6)65,000
12/31/02	
Bal 10,000	

Supplies

Dr +	Cr -
12/31/01 Bal 8,000	(10)5,000
12/31/02 Bal 3,000	

Building

Dr+	Cr-
12/31/01 Bal 54,000	(12)6,000
12/31/02 Bal 48,000	

Land

Dr+	Cr-
(3)20,000	
12/31/02 Bal 20,000	

Accounts Payable

Dr-	Cr+
	12/31/01 10,000 Bal
(8)65,000	(4) 75,000
65,000	85,000
	12/31/02 20,000 Bal

Salaries Payable

Dr-	Cr+
(1)16,000	12/31/01 16,000 Bal

Notes Payable

Dr-	Cr+
	(2) 25,000
	12/31/02 25,000 Bal

Income Tax Payable

	(14) 12,000
	12/31/02 12,000 Bal

Capital Stock

Dr-	Cr+
	12/31/01 100,000 Bal
	12/31/02 100,000 Bal

Retained Earnings

Dr-	Cr+
	12/31/01 20,000 Bal

Dividends

Dr-	Cr+
(15)18,000	
12/31/02 18,000 Bal	

Income Statement Accounts

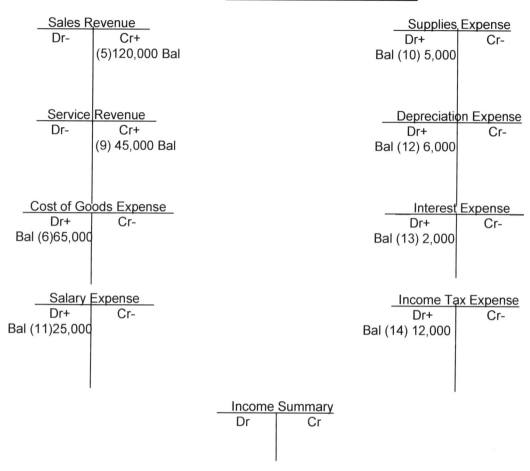

Sales Revenue

Dr-	Cr+
	(5)120,000 Bal

Service Revenue

Dr-	Cr+
	(9) 45,000 Bal

Cost of Goods Expense

Dr+	Cr-
Bal (6)65,000	

Salary Expense

Dr+	Cr-
Bal (11)25,000	

Supplies Expense

Dr+	Cr-
Bal (10) 5,000	

Depreciation Expense

Dr+	Cr-
Bal (12) 6,000	

Interest Expense

Dr+	Cr-
Bal (13) 2,000	

Income Tax Expense

Dr+	Cr-
Bal (14) 12,000	

Income Summary

Dr	Cr

A trial balance can now be prepared from the previous ledger balances.

APEX Corp.
Trial Balance
Dec. 31, 2002

Debit Balances		Credit Balances	
Cash	$84,000	Accounts Payable	$20,000
Accounts Receivable	44,000	Notes Payable	25,000
Inventory	10,000	Income Tax Payable	12,000
Supplies	3,000	Capital Stock	100,000
Building	48,000	Retained Earnings	20,000
Land	20,000	Sales Revenue	120,000
Cost of Goods Sold Expense	65,000	Service Revenue	45,000
Salary Expense	25,000		
Supplies Expense	5,000		
Depreciation Expense	6,000		
Interest Expense	2,000		
Income Tax Expense	12,000		
Dividends	18,000		
Total	$342,000	Total	$342,000

Income Statement and Balance Sheet

The Income Statement, Statement of Retained Earnings, and Balance Sheet will now be prepared from the preceding trial balance. (The arrows are included to highlight the linkage between the statements.)

APEX Corp.
Income Statement
For the year ended, Dec. 31, 2002

Sales Revenue		$120,000
Service Revenue		45,000
Total Revenue		$165,000
Expenses:		
Cost of Goods Sold	$65,000	
Salary Expense	25,000	
Supplies Expense	5,000	
Depreciation Expense	6,000	
Interest Expense	2,000	
		103,000
Net Income before Income Taxes		$62,000
Income Tax Expense		12,000
Net Income		$50,000

APEX Corp.
Statement of Retained Earnings
For the year ended, Dec. 31, 2002

Retained Earnings, 1/1/02	$20,000
Net Income	50,000
	$70,000
Dividends	18,000
Retained Earnings, 12/31/02	$52,000

APEX Corp.
Balance Sheet
Dec. 31, 2002

Assets			Liabilities and Owners' Equity		
Current Assets			**Current Liabilities**		
Cash	$84,000		Accounts Payable	$20,000	
Accounts Receivable	44,000		Income Tax Payable	12,000	
Inventory	10,000			$32,000	
Supplies	3,000		**Long-Term Liabilities**		
	$141,000		Notes Payable	25,000	
				$57,000	
Fixed Assets					
Building	$48,000		**Owners' Equity**		
Land	20,000		Capital Stock	$100,000	
	$68,000		Retained Earnings	52,000	
				152,000	
			Total Liabilities and		
Total Assets	$209,000		Owners' Equity	$209,000	

The above balance sheet is in what is known as "classified" form. It breaks down the assets into current and fixed and the liabilities into current and long-term. Current assets are cash and those assets which have a short-term life span. Fixed assets are long-lived assets not normally intended for sale.

Current liabilities are those liabilities which will normally be liquidated in the short-term, while Long-term liabilities will come due further in the future.

Cash Flow Statement[2]

The Income Statement as discussed in Chapter Three shows net asset increases and decreases resulting from operations of the business. What it fails to show is the company's cash flow activity. To fill this void, the Cash Flow Statement is prepared which shows the sources from which cash was received, the uses to which cash was put, and the net change in cash for the year.

The Statement shows cash flow from three types of activity: Operating, Investing, and Financing. For the operating section of the statement the most widely used form of presentation is the "indirect" form which starts with net income (or loss) as shown in the income statement and adjusts it to show cash flow from operating activity.[3]

---

[2] This is the commonly used name for this statement. In a formal presentation, it would be labeled The Statement of Changes in Financial Condition.

[3] There is an alternate "direct" form of presentation for the operating section of the Cash Flow Statement which does not reconcile net income to cash flow from operations but rather shows the cash flow related to the individual components of the Income Statement and the resulting net impact on cash. Appendix C illustrates this alternate form of the Statement.

Illustration I which follows presents a short guide to preparing the <u>operating section</u> of the cash flow statement under the indirect method. In it, the increases and decreases to which reference is made are determined from the beginning and ending ledger account balances for the year covered by the statement.

Illustration I
Cash Flow Statement
Operating Section Preparation: Indirect Method

Net Income	$xxx
1. <u>Add</u> cash receipts not included in net income determination as indicated by:	
A. Decrease in receivables related to operations.	xx
2. <u>Subtract</u> non-cash revenues included positively in net income determination as indicated by:	
A. Increase in receivables related to operations.	(xx)
3. <u>Subtract</u> cash payments not included in net income determination as indicated by:	
A. Increase in inventory and/or supplies	(xx)
B. Decrease in payables related to operations.	(xx)
4. <u>Add</u> non-cash expenses included negatively in net income determination as indicated by:	
A. Decrease in inventory and/or supplies	xx
B. Increase in payables related to operations	xx
C. Other non-cash expenses such as depreciation.	xx
Increase (or decrease) in cash from operating activity	$xxx(or xxx)

Note: This Illustration does not include all the possible adjustments to net income which might be made to convert it to cash flow from operating activity. It does cover the most common ones.

Using Illustration I as a guide and including investing and financing activities, the cash flow statement for the APEX Corp. would be as shown below. (Notes: The increases and decreases for the accounts for the year are determined from the previously presented beginning and ending ledger account balances for the year 2002. The numbered letters in parentheses correlate the statement to Illustration I.)

APEX Corp.
Cash Flow Statement
For the year ended Dec. 31, 2002

Cash flow from operating activity:

Net income	$50,000
Increase in accounts receivable (2A)	(20,000)
Increase in inventory (3A)	(10,000)
Decrease in supplies (4A)	5,000
Increase in accounts payable (4B)	10,000
Decrease in salaries payable (3B)	(16,000)
Increase in income tax payable (4B)	12,000
Depreciation (4C)	6,000
Increase in cash from operating activity	$37,000

Cash flow from investing activity:

Purchase of land	(20,000)

Cash flow from financing activity:

Borrowing on note payable	25,000
Dividends paid	(18,000)
Net increase in cash	$24,000

Closing Entries

At this point, the following closing entries would be recorded for the APEX Corp.

(C$_1$)	Dr: Sales Revenue	$120,000	
	Dr: Service Revenue	45,000	
	Cr: Income Summary		$165,000
(C$_2$)	Dr: Income Summary	$115,000	
	Cr: Cost of Goods Sold Expense		$65,000
	Cr: Salary Expense		25,000
	Cr: Supplies Expense		5,000
	Cr: Depreciation Expense		6,000
	Cr: Interest Expense		2,000
	Cr: Income tax Expense		12,000
(C$_3$)	Dr: Income Summary (for net income)	$50,000	
	Cr: Retained Earnings		$50,000
(C$_4$)	Dr: Retained Earnings	$18,000	
	Cr: Dividends		$18,000

After the closing entries are posted, the revenue, expense, income summary, and dividends accounts would be closed to zero balances and the retained earnings account would appear as follows:

	Retained Earnings		
	Dr-	Cr+	
		12/31/01	20,000 Bal
(C$_4$) Dividends 18,000		(C$_3$) Net Income	50,000
18,000			70,000
		12/31/02	52,000 Bal

All balance sheet accounts would now have ending balances which would become the beginning balances of 2003. This now concludes the APEX Corp. example.

Three Appendices follow which discuss accounting for merchandise inventory under the periodic inventory method, the Matching Concept, and preparation of the Cash Flow Statement using the direct method. Two exercises then conclude the chapter.

Appendix A

Periodic Inventory Method

In the APEX Corp. example, the "perpetual" inventory method was used. The hallmark of this method is the recording of the cost of the inventory sold at the time of the sale. The alternate "periodic" inventory method delays such recording until the end of the accounting period. At that time a physical count and pricing of the ending inventory is performed and cost of goods sold is developed and recorded. For comparison, the two methods are illustrated below using the information from the APEX Corp. example.

Journal Entries

Perpetual	**Periodic**

Entry (4) Inventory for future sale is purchased on credit for $75,000.

Perpetual	Periodic

Dr: Inventory (+A) $75,000
   Cr: Accounts Payable(+L) $75,000
	Dr: Purchases $75,000
	   (temporary account)
	       Cr: Accounts Payable(+L) $75,000

Entry (5) Inventory is sold to customers on credit for $120,000

Perpetual	Periodic

Dr: Accounts Receivable(+A) $120,000
   Cr: Sales Revenue(+R+NI+OE) $120,000
	Dr: Accounts Receivable(+A)$120,000
	   Cr: Sales Revenue(+R+NI+OE)$120,000

Entry (6) The cost of the inventory sold in 5 was $65,000

Perpetual	Periodic
Dr: Cost of Goods Sold Expense(+E-NI-OE) $65,000 Cr: Inventory(-A) $65,000	No Entry

At the end of the period, cost of goods sold expense and the amount of the ending inventory are developed under the periodic method by the following calculation.

Calculation:

Beginning Inventory 12/31/01	0
+Purchases	$75,000
Cost of Goods Available for Sale	$75,000
-Ending Inventory 12/31/02 (this amount comes from the physical counting and pricing of the ending inventory at cost)	-10,000
Cost of Goods Sold Expense	$65,000

The foregoing calculation would now be used under the periodic method to make a reclassification entry to record the ending inventory and cost of goods sold expense as follows:

Entry (7) Dr: Inventory 12/31/02 (+A) $10,000(To)◄──────────┐
       Dr: Cost of Goods Sold Expense(+E-NI-OE)$65,000(To) ◄────────┐   │
        Cr: Purchases (to close) $75,000(From) ──►│
        Cr: Inventory 12/31/01 (to close)   0(From) ──►
          (usually there will be a
          beginning inventory balance
          to close out.)

Ledger Accounts

After posting the above entries, the ledger accounts related to inventory for both methods would appear as follows. (The numbers in parentheses refer to the preceding journal entries.)

Perpetual			Periodic	
Inventory			**Inventory**	
12/31/01 Bal 0		12/31/01 Bal 0	(7) 0
(4) 75,000	(6) 65,000	12/31/02(7)Bal 10,000	
12/31/02 Bal 10,000			

Cost of Goods Sold Expense			Cost of Goods Sold Expense	
(6) 65,000			(7) 65,000	

Purchases	
(4) 75,000	(7) 75,000

Appendix B

The Matching Concept

The matching concept relates to accounting for the expired embodied costs (expenses) that are to be shown as deductions from revenue in a given period's income statement. The general principle is that a cost should be matched (as an expense) against the revenue of the period(s) with which it has a <u>cause and effect</u> relationship. That is, the cost is seen as the input effort which caused the accomplishment, revenue. Note that the cost expiration can relate solely to the revenue of one period in which case it is <u>separate</u> to that period. It can also be that the cost is related to the revenues of more than one period; in which case it is <u>common</u> (or joint) to those periods. There is also the possibility that the expired cost is not related to any period's revenue whatsoever. In this case, resort would be made to <u>expedient</u> matching which would consider the cost to be expired in the period its loss of utility was discovered. To summarize, under the matching concept an expired cost can be matched against revenue of a given period in the following ways:

1. Cause and Effect/ Separate (Example: Inventory)
2. Cause and Effect/Common (Joint) (Example: Fixed Asset)
3. Expedient (Example: Loss from Damage)

The matching methods available for Inventory and Fixed Assets will now be examined briefly.

Inventory Costs

When inventory is acquired, certain decisions concerning accounting for it must be made. First, as seen in the Appendix A to this chapter, a choice has to be made between the <u>perpetual</u> and <u>periodic</u> methods. After this decision has been made the following question arises: What inventory cost should be matched against revenue as cost of goods sold expense when the goods are sold? This type of matching is on a <u>cause and effect/separate</u> basis and there are four possibilities to choose from. These "cost flow" choices are:

1. Specifically identify as expense the cost of items sold
2. Use the cost of the earliest items acquired as the cost of goods sold expense (First-In, First-Out or FIFO)
3. Use an average cost of the acquired items as the cost of goods sold expense
4. Use the cost of the latest items acquired as the cost of goods sold expense (Last-In, First-Out or LIFO)

Specific Identification (Method 1) coupled with perpetual records would be appropriate for companies dealing in heterogeneous, high value items such as cars, yachts, etc.

For homogeneous relatively low priced items, one of the other three cost flow methods would be chosen and combined with either the perpetual or periodic method. Therefore, for these items, six possibilities exist for matching their cost against revenue as cost of goods sold expense. These are:

1. Perpetual FIFO
2. Perpetual Average
3. Perpetual LIFO
4. Periodic FIFO
5. Periodic Average
6. Periodic LIFO

A detailed discussion of the above six methods is beyond the scope of this book. The reader is referred to any accounting textbook for computational illustrations of each method.

Fixed Assets

The matching of the cost of fixed assets against revenue as depreciation expense is on a <u>cause and effect</u> basis with the cost being <u>common</u> (joint) to more than one period's revenue. Therefore, the expiration of the fixed asset cost is recorded as depreciation expense over several periods of expected use and benefit. Any systematic and rational cost allocation method is acceptable for computing the depreciation per year.

A commonly used depreciation method is <u>straight-line</u> which presumes equal asset utilization and benefit each year. This results in a constant amount of depreciation expense each year (as was shown in the previous Apex Corp. example). It might be; however, that most of the use and benefit of the fixed asset is expected to fall in the early years. In such case, "high to low" depreciation expense would be recorded with the amount of depreciation taken each year decreasing. For this type of "accelerated" depreciation, <u>declining balance</u> and <u>sum-of-years digits</u> methods are available. Although seldom used, "low to high" depreciation methods which increase the depreciation each year can also be used if the fixed asset's use and benefit is expected to increase over time. The reader is referred to any accounting text for computational illustrations of the above mentioned depreciation methods.

Appendix C

<u>Cash Flow Statement: Direct Method</u>
The Cash Flow Statement shown previously in the APEX Corp. example utilized the "indirect" method which adjusts net income to cash flow from operations. An equally acceptable alternative is the "direct" method which shows the cash flow related to each component of the income statement and the net result. Illustration I which follows presents a short guide to preparing the <u>operating section</u> of the cash flow statement under the <u>direct</u> method. Then, the cash flow statement for the APEX Corp. is shown in direct form. (The numbered letters in parentheses in the APEX Statement correlate it to Illustration I.)

Illustration I
Cash Flow Statement
Operating Section Preparation: Direct Method

<u>Sales and Other Revenues</u>	$xxx
1. <u>Add</u>: cash receipts not included in revenues as indicated by:	
A. Decrease in receivables related to operations	xx
2. <u>Subtract</u>: non-cash revenue included in revenues as indicated by:	
A. Increase in receivables related to operations	(xx)
Cash Inflow	$xxx
<u>Cost of Goods Sold and Other Expenses</u>	$xxx
3. <u>Add</u>: cash payments not included in expenses as indicated by:	
A. Increase in inventory and/or supplies	xx
B. Decrease in payables related to operations	xx
4. <u>Subtract</u>: non-cash expenses included in expenses as indicated by:	
A. Decrease in inventory and/or supplies	(xx)
B. Increase in payables related to operations	(xx)
C. Other non-cash expenses such as depreciation	(xx)
Cash Outflow	-$xxx
Increase (or decrease) in cash from operating activity	$xxx (or xxx)

APEX Corp.
Cash Flow Statement
For the year ended Dec. 31, 2002

Cash Flow from operating activity:

Sales	$120,000	
Increase in accounts receivable (2A)	(20,000)	$100,000
Service Revenue		$45,000
Cash Inflow		$145,000
Cost of Goods Sold	$65,000	
Increase in inventory (3A)	10,000	
Increase in accounts payable (4B)	(10,000)	$65,000
Supplies Expense	$5,000	
Decrease in supplies (4A)	(5,000)	-0-
Salary Expense	$25,000	
Decrease in salaries payable (3B)	16,000	41,000
Interest Expense		2,000
Income Tax Expense	$12,000	
Increase in income tax payable (4B)	(12,000)	-0-
Cash Outflow		$108,000
Increase in cash from operating activity		$37,000

Cash flow from investing activity:

Purchase of land	(20,000)

Cash flow from financing activity:

Borrowing on note payable	25,000
Dividends paid	(18,000)
Net increase in cash	$24,000

Exercise 1 Journal Entries and Effects

For each of the statements below give the journal entry, without amounts. After each account debited and credited, indicate its effect (+ or -) on net income NI, assets A, liabilities L, and owners' equity OE.(The company uses the perpetual inventory method.)

Example: Merchandise inventory is purchased on credit.

Dr: Inventory (+A)
Cr: Accounts Payable (+L)

1. The accounts payable above is paid.

2. Sales entry is made for merchandise sold on credit.

3. Cost of goods sold expense related to 2 is recorded.

4. Accounts receivable from 2 are collected.

5. Income tax owed is recorded.

6. Income tax recorded in 5 is paid.

7. A dividend to stockholders is paid (a dividends account is used.)

8. Make the entry to close the dividends account to retained earnings. (Omit effects for the entry.)

Exercise 1 Solution

1. Dr: Accounts Payable (-L)
   Cr: Cash (-A)

2. Dr: Accounts Receivable (+A)
   Cr: Sales Revenue (+NI+OE)

3. Dr: Cost of Goods Sold Expense (-NI-OE)
   Cr: Inventory (-A)

4. Dr: Cash (+A)
   Cr: Accounts Receivable (-A)

5. Dr: Income Tax Expense (-NI-OE)
   Cr: Income Tax Payable (+L)

6. Dr: Income Tax Payable (-L)
   Cr: Cash (-A)

7. Dr: Dividends (-RE –OE)
   Cr: Cash (-A)

8. Dr: Retained Earnings
   Cr: Dividends

Exercise 2 Cash Flow Statement

From the data given below, prepare a cash flow statement using the indirect method. Use the answer sheet provided on the next page.

Data

Operating Activity:

Net income for 2002	$90,000
Increase in accounts receivable	70,000
Decrease in other receivables	2,000
Decrease in inventory	15,000
Decrease in accounts payable	20,000
Increase in salaries payable	5,000
Depreciation expense	8,000

Investing Activity:

1. Land held as an investment was sold for cash at its book value of $35,000.

Financing Activity:

1. Additional capital stock was issued to owners for $50,000 cash.
2. A dividend of $20,000 was paid to owners.

Cash Flow Statement
For the year ended Dec. 31, 2002

Cash flow from operating activity:
    Net income $90,000
    Increase in accounts receivable
    Decrease in other receivables
    Decrease in inventory
    Decrease in accounts payable
    Increase in salaries payable
    Depreciation expense   _____
    Increase (Decrease) in cash from operating activity

Cash flow from investing activity:

Cash flow from financing activity:

Net increase (decrease) in cash   _____

What problem does the operating section of the cash flow statement show the company is having?

Exercise 2 Solution

Cash Flow Statement
For the year ended Dec. 31, 2002

Cash flow from operating activity:	
Net income	$90,000
Increase in accounts receivable	(70,000)
Decrease in other receivables	2,000
Decrease in inventory	15,000
Decrease in accounts payable	(20,000)
Increase in salaries payable	5,000
Depreciation expense	8,000
Increase (Decrease) in cash from operating activity	$30,000
Cash flow from investing activity:	
Sale of land	35,000
Cash flow from financing activity:	
Issuance of capital stock	50,000
Dividend paid	(20,000)
Net increase (decrease) in cash	$95,000

The company is apparently experiencing a collection problem with accounts receivable.

Chapter Five

Other Exchanges and Accounts I

This chapter examines two types of exchanges not covered in the preceding APEX Corp. example. These are continuous exchanges involving accruals and prepayments, and gain and loss exchanges.

Accruals and Prepayments

The usual perception of an exchange is that it occurs at a specific point in time. This of course is true for many exchanges; however, some exchanges occur on continuous basis over time.[XIII] These exchanges involve the receipt and giving of services such as: insurance (risk coverage), utilities (heat, light, power), rent (occupancy), interest (use of money), taxes (government services), and salaries and wages (employee services). Payment for these services can be made either <u>after</u> the service is provided or <u>before</u>.

If payment is made <u>after</u> the service is provided, the expense accumulates, i.e., <u>accrues</u>, to the date of payment. At that time, the expense and cash payment are recorded. However, a problem arises when financial statements are to be prepared at the end of an accounting period prior to cash payment. In such a case, an accrual adjusting entry must be made to record the accumulated service expense and the amount owed for it. As an example assume a customer is charged $400 a month for electricity. Service is started on Dec. 15, 2001, financial statements are to be prepared on Dec. 31, 2001, and payment is to be made on Jan. 15, 2002. The customer's entries in December and January are shown below (with parenthetical explanatory comments included.)

Customer's entries

12/15/01	<u>Service started</u> No journal entry made; notation made of $400 per month charge

12/31/01   <u>Accrual adjustment for December services received</u>
           Dr: Electricity Expense (-NI-OE) $200
             (electricity received in Dec.)
                Cr: Payable (+L) $200
                  (obligation given to utility co.)

1/15/02   <u>January service received and cash paid</u>
           Dr: Electricity Expense (-NI-OE) $200
             (electricity received in Jan.)
           Dr: Payable (-L) $200
             (release from obligation
              to utility co. received)
                Cr: Cash (given) (-A) $400

The utility company which provided the service to the customer discussed above faces a similar adjustment problem at Dec. 31, 2001 with regard to the recording of accrued revenue. The entries for the utility company are shown below.

Utility Co. entries

12/15/01	Service started No journal entry made; notation made of $400 per month charge		

12/31/01	Accrual adjustment for December service given
	Dr: Receivable (+A)
	   (claim against customer
	    received)
	      Cr: Service Revenue (+NI +OE)
	      (electricity given in Dec.)
		$200	$200

1/15/02	January service given and cash received
	Dr: Cash (received) (+A)
	      Cr: Service Revenue (+NI+OE)
	      (electricity given in Jan.)
	      Cr: Receivable (-A)
	      (release from claim against
	      customer given)
		$400	$200
			
			$200

As mentioned previously, payment can also precede the providing of service. In such a case, the accounting would involve a prepaid expense asset for the one to receive the service and an unearned revenue liability for the one to give the service. Just as with accruals, an end of the period adjustment problem exists in connection with these items. The example used above will now be repeated to show the accounting assuming payment for the service is made in advance.

Customer's entries

12/15/01	Cash paid and one month's service started
	Dr: Prepaid Electricity Expense (+A)
	   (claim against utility co. received)
	      Cr: Cash (given) (-A)
		$400	$400

12/31/01	Prepaid asset adjustment for Dec. service received
	Dr: Electricity Expense (-NI-OE)
	   (electricity received in Dec.)
	      Cr: Prepaid Electricity Expense (-A)
	      (release from claim against
	      utility co. given)
		$200	$200

1/15/02	January service received	
	Dr: Electricity Expense (-NI-OE)	$200
	(electricity received in Jan.)	
	Cr: Prepaid Electricity Expense (-A)	$200
	(release from claim against utility co. given)	

In the above example, be sure to recognize that the prepaid expense asset is actually a receivable claim due in service rather than cash. The utility company's entries for the revenue side of the above example will now be presented.

Utility Co. entries

12/15/01	Cash received and one month's service started	
	Dr: Cash (received) (+A)	$400
	Cr: Unearned Revenue (+L)	$400
	(obligation given to customer)	

12/31/01	Unearned liability adjustment for Dec. service given	
	Dr: Unearned Revenue (-L)	$200
	(release from obligation to customer received)	
	Cr: Service Revenue (+NI +OE)	$200
	(electricity given in Dec.)	

1/15/02	January service given	
	Dr: Unearned Revenue (-L)	$200
	(release from obligation to customer received)	
	Cr: Service Revenue (+NI+OE)	$200
	(electricity given in Jan.)	

In the above example, be sure to recognize that the unearned revenue liability is actually a payable obligation owed in service rather than cash.

Gains and Losses

Before discussing gains and losses in detail a few general observations about them will be made. Gains have the same impact on the financial statements as revenue in that they increase net income in the income statement which in turn increases retained earnings and therefore total owner's equity in the balance sheet. Conversely, losses have the same financial statement impact as expenses in that they decrease net income, retained earnings and total owner's equity. Also, gains and losses are closed out at the end of the accounting period in the same manner as revenues and expenses. Some specific gain and loss situations will now be examined.

One type of loss is a "lost cost" which arises from theft, destruction, or obsolescence of unexpired cost assets such as inventory, buildings, and equipment. The journal entry for such a loss is a reclassification which transfers the amount of the loss <u>from</u> the asset <u>to</u> a loss account. As an example, the entry for a $1,000 loss due to inventory obsolescence would be:

Dr: Loss from Inventory Obsolescence (-NI-OE)(To)	**$1,000**
Cr: Inventory (-A) (From)	**$1,000**

Gains and losses are also recorded in connection with the sale of fixed assets such as land, buildings, and equipment.[1] A gain on the sale of a fixed asset occurs when the asset is sold for more than its book value (i.e., the amount of its account balance). Such a gain causes an increase in the entity's obligation to its owners which is implemented through inclusion of the gain in the income statement as a positive element in the determination of net income.[2]

As an example of a gain on the sale of a fixed asset, assume land with a book value of $10,000 is sold for $12,000. The gain exchange entry would be:

Dr: Cash (received) (+A)	**$12,000**
Cr: Land (-A)	**$10,000**
(book value of land	
given to buyer)	
Cr: Gain on sale (+NI+OE)	**$2,000**
(obligation to owners given)	

In the case of a loss on the sale of a fixed asset, the loss decreases the entity's obligation to owners through its inclusion in the income statement as a negative element in the determination of net income.

As an example, assume land with a book value of $10,000 is sold for $7,000. The loss exchange entry would be:

Dr: Cash (received) (+A)	**$7,000**
Dr: Loss on sale (-NI-OE)	**3,000**
(release from obligation	
to owners received)	
Cr: Land (-A)	**$10,000**
(book value of land	
given to buyer)	

---

[1] Revenue and expense accounts are not used for these items since they are not the entity's normal stock-in-trade.
[2] In the past, some of the gains (losses) discussed in this section were credited (debited) directly to owners' equity rather than being channeled through the income statement. This practice has been eliminated by current accounting standards.

Gains and losses similar to those arising from the sale of fixed assets can also occur in connection with the settlement of financial claims and obligations. For example, assume a debt in the form of a $10,000 note is settled for $9,000 by mutual agreement between the borrower and lender.

The entries for the debt settlement on the books of both parties would be as follows:

Borrower's entries

    Dr: Note Payable (-L) $10,000
        (release from obligation to lender received)
            Cr: Cash (given) (-A) $9,000
            Cr: Gain on debt settlement (+NI+OE) $1,000
                (obligation to owners given)

Lender's entries

    Dr: Cash (received) (+A) $9,000
    Dr: Loss on debt settlement(-NI-OE) $1,000
        (release from obligation to owners received)
            Cr: Note Receivable (-A) $10,000
                (release from claim against borrower given)

On the other hand, if the preceding debt was settled for $11,000 because the borrower elected to pay a prepayment penalty, the entries would be:

Borrower's entries

    Dr: Note Payable (-L) $10,000
        (release from obligation to lender received)
    Dr: Loss on debt settlement (-NI-OE) $1,000
        (release from obligation to owners received)
            Cr: Cash (given) (-A) $11,000

Lender's entries

    Dr: Cash (received) (+A) $11,000
            Cr: Note Receivable (-A) $10,000
                (release from claim against borrower given)
            Cr: Gain on debt settlement (+NI+OE) $1,000
                (obligation to owners given)

It should be noted that the gain and loss entries shown previously for fixed asset sales and debt settlement are not the normal bilateral (two-party) exchanges between the entity and one other party. They are what can be called trilateral (three-party) exchanges because they involve the entity, a non-owner, and the entity's owners.[XIV] Using assumed figures these exchanges can be depicted as follows:

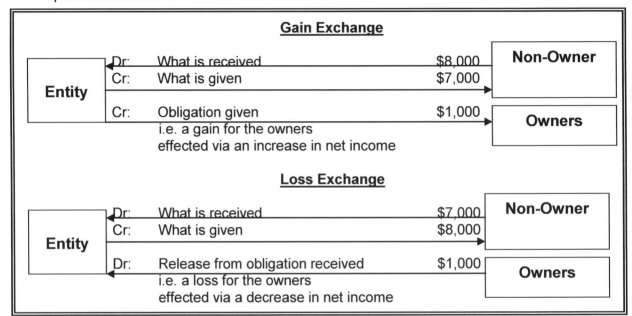

Gain Exchange

Dr:	What is received	$8,000	**Non-Owner**	
Cr:	What is given	$7,000		

Entity

Cr:	Obligation given	$1,000	**Owners**
	i.e. a gain for the owners		
	effected via an increase in net income		

Loss Exchange

Dr:	What is received	$7,000	**Non-Owner**
Cr:	What is given	$8,000	

Entity

Dr:	Release from obligation received	$1,000	**Owners**
	i.e. a loss for the owners		
	effected via a decrease in net income		

Before leaving gains and losses be sure to recognize that their inclusion in the income statement expands its content to the following:

Income Statement

Revenue
+ Gains
- Expenses
- Losses
‾‾‾‾‾‾‾‾‾‾‾‾‾‾‾‾‾‾‾‾
= Net Income (or Net Loss)

Also, don't forget the two exercises which follow.

Exercise 1 Journal Entries and Effects

For each of the numbered items below, make the required journal entry. After each debit and each credit, indicate parenthetically the effect it would have on: Net Income (NI), Assets (A), Liabilities (L), and Owners' Equity (OE).

Example: At June 30, 2002, a $3,000 accrual adjustment was made for 3 days wages owed to employees at month end.

    Dr: Wages Expense (-NI-OE) $3,000
        Cr: Wages Payable (+L) $3,000

1. The employees in the example above were paid a full 5-day week's wages of $5,000 on July 2, 2002.

2. At the beginning of a month, the company paid two-months' rent on a building in advance. The amount was $8,000.

3. One-half of the rent paid in advance in 2 above is recorded as an expense at the end of the month.

4. The company owning the building in 2 above received the $8,000 rent in advance at the beginning of the month.

5. One-half of the rent received in advance in 4 above is recorded as revenue at the end of the month.

6. On Dec. 31, a $500 receivable for 10 days accrued interest earned but not yet collected was recorded.

7. The interest in 6 above was collected in January of the next year as a part of a total $1,500 received for 30 days interest earned.

8. An uninsured fire loss occurred which destroyed inventory having a book value of $9,000.

9. Land with a book value of $40,000 was sold for $45,000 cash.

10. Another parcel of land with a book value of $60,000 was sold for $58,000 cash.

11. $4,000 was accepted from an insolvent debtor in full payment of a $5,000 note receivable.

12. The company was able to settle a $2,500 accounts payable that it owed for a cash payment of $2,000.

13. The company paid $8,400 to eliminate a $8,000 note payable having a high interest rate.

14. The holder of the $8,000 note in 13 recorded receipt of the $8,400 redemption payment.

Exercise 1 Solution

1. Dr: Wages Payable (-L) $3,000
   Dr: Wages Expense (-NI-OE) $2,000
       Cr: Cash (-A) $5,000

2. Dr: Prepaid Rent Expense (+A) $8,000
       Cr: Cash (-A) $8,000

3. Dr: Rent Expense (-NI-OE) $4,000
       Cr: Prepaid Rent Expense (-A) $4,000

4. Dr: Cash (+A) $8,000
       Cr: Unearned Rent Revenue (+L) $8,000

5. Dr: Unearned Rent Revenue (-L) $4,000
       Cr: Rent Revenue (+NI+OE) $4,000

6. Dr: Interest Receivable (+A) $500
       Cr: Interest Revenue (+NI+OE) $500

7. Dr: Cash (+A) $1,500
       Cr: Interest Receivable (-A) $500
       Cr: Interest Revenue (+NI+OE) $1,000

8. Dr: Fire Loss (-NI-OE) $9,000
       Cr: Inventory (-A) $9,000

9. Dr: Cash (+A) $45,000
       Cr: Land (-A) $40,000
       Cr: Gain on sale (+NI+OE) $5,000

10. Dr: Cash (+A) $58,000
    Dr: Loss on sale (-NI-OE) $2,000
        Cr: Land (-A) $60,000

11. Dr: Cash (+A) $4,000
    Dr: Loss on debt settlement (-NI-OE) $1,000
       Cr: Note Receivable (-A) $5,000

12. Dr: Accounts Payable (-L) $2,500
       Cr: Cash (-A) $2,000
       Cr: Gain on debt settlement (+NI+OE) $500

13. Dr: Note Payable (-L) $8,000
    Dr: Loss on debt settlement (-NI-OE) $400
       Cr: Cash (-A) $8,400

14. Dr: Cash (+A) $8,400
       Cr: Note Receivable (-A) $8,000
       Cr: Gain on debt settlement (+NI+OE) $400

Exercise 2 Financial Statements and Closing Entries

From the following alphabetical listing of account balances, prepare an Income Statement and Statement of Retained Earnings and make closing entries.

('000 omitted)

Dividends	$ 60
Expenses	130
Gain	50
Loss	20
Retained Earnings (beginning balance)	70
Revenue	200

Exercise 2 Solution

Income Statement

Revenue		$200
Gain		50
		$250
Expenses	130	
Loss	20	(150)
Net Income		$100

Statement of Retained Earnings

Retained Earnings (beginning)	$ 70
+Net Income	100
	$170
-Dividends	(60)
Retained Earnings (ending)	$110

Closing Entries

1.	Dr: Revenue	$200	
	Dr: Gain	$ 50	
	Cr: Income Summary		$250
2.	Dr: Income Summary	$150	
	Cr: Expenses		$130
	Cr: Loss		$ 20
3.	Dr: Income Summary	$100	
	Cr: Retained Earnings		$100
4.	Dr: Retained Earnings	$ 60	
	Cr: Dividends		$ 60

Chapter Six
Other Exchanges and Accounts II

This concluding chapter discusses the use of contra and adjunct accounts and the question of recording contractual exchanges. An Appendix that discusses current value reporting is also included.

Contra and Adjunct Accounts

A contra account is an auxiliary account which is deducted from a primary account to which it is related. Several types of contra accounts can appear in the financial statements. In the income statement, a common one is Sales Discounts which is deducted from Sales Revenue. This account is typically used when a company rewards a credit customer with a discount for prompt payment. For example, assume a sale of $5,000 is made to a customer with a provision that a 4% discount will be allowed if the customer remits within a certain period of time. Assuming the customer does so, the selling company's entries would be:

Original sale

Dr: Accounts Receivable	$5,000	
Cr: Sales Revenue		$5,000

Payment is received within the discount period

Dr: Cash	$4,800	
Dr: Sales Discount (Sales reduction account)	$200	
(.04 x $5,000)		
Cr: Accounts Receivable		$5,000

The income statement presentation would be:

Sales (gross)	$5,000	
Less Sales Discounts	(200)	
Net Sales	$4,800	

On the asset side of the balance sheet, a common contra account is Allowance for Uncollectible Accounts which is set up in anticipation of some customers defaulting on their accounts receivable. The amount recorded is an estimate based on the company's prior accounts receivable collection experience. An example of the accounting is shown next.

---

1. Sales of $20,000 are made to various customers on credit.

Dr: Accounts Receivable   **$20,000**
    Cr: Sales Revenue   **$20,000**

2. Uncollectible accounts are estimated at 5% of sales.

Dr: Uncollectible Account Expense   **$1,000**
    Cr: Allowance for Uncollectible Accounts   **$1,000**
    (Accounts Receivable reduction account)

(Note: The uncollectible account "expense" debited in the above entry is not actually an expense since it does not represent expired goods or services. Rather, it is a financial loss resulting from the uncollectibility of claims held. However, expense is the common term used and it does little harm to use it instead of loss since the effect on net income is the same.)

If a balance sheet were to be prepared after entries 1 and 2, it would show:

Assets

Accounts Receivable (gross)	$20,000
Less Allowance for Uncollectible Accounts	(1,000)
Accounts Receivable (net)	$19,000

---

3. The account of Customer X for $200 is written off as uncollectible.

Dr: Allowance for Uncollectible Accounts   **$200**
    Cr: Accounts Receivable (Customer X)   **$200**

The above entry would have no effect on the company's total assets. Both Accounts Receivable and the Allowance account would be reduced by $200 but the net accounts receivable asset would still stand at $19,000 as shown below.

Assets

Accounts Receivable (gross)	$19,800
Less Allowance for Uncollectible Accounts	(800)
Accounts Receivable (net)	$19,000

Another common contra asset account is Accumulated Depreciation. In the entries for depreciation shown in previous chapters, the credit for the cost expiration was made directly to the asset being depreciated. This is acceptable; however, it has the drawback of obscuring the original cost of the asset and the amount of depreciation taken on it to date. Using an accumulated depreciation contra account permits this information to be shown separately in the accounts. As an example, recall in Chapter Two a small building was purchased for $60,000 and depreciated over a 10 year life by the straight line method. If an accumulated depreciation account had been used, the journal entries and financial statement presentation for the first two years would have been as follows:

Year 1 Purchase of building for $60,000 cash.

Dr: Building	$60,000	
Cr. Cash		$60,000

Depreciation entry for Year 1.

Dr: Depreciation Expense	$6,000	
Cr: Accumulated Depreciation		$6,000
(Building reduction account)		

Assets

Building (cost)	$60,000
Less Accumulated Depreciation	(6,000)
Building (book value)	$54,000

Year 2 Depreciation entry for Year 2.

Dr: Depreciation Expense	$6,000	
Cr: Accumulated Depreciation		$6,000

Assets

Building (cost)	$60,000
Less Accumulated Depreciation	(12,000)
Building (book value)	$48,000

Now assume the building in the preceding example was sold for $51,000 cash just after depreciation for year 2 was recorded. Since the book value of the building is now $48,000, this would result is a gain of $3,000 and the sales entry would be:

Dr: Cash	$51,000	
Dr: Accumulated Depreciation*	$12,000	
Cr: Building *		$60,000
Cr: Gain on sale		$3,000

As an assumed alternative, if the above sale of the building had been for $45,000 the entry would be:

Dr: Cash	$45,000	
Dr: Accumulated Depreciation	$12,000	
Dr: Loss on sale	$3,000	
Cr: Building		$60,000

---

* In the above entry, the net effect if the $12,000 debit to accumulated depreciation and the $60,000 credit to building is to decrease assets by the $48,000 book value at which the building had been carried.

Contra accounts can also be used in conjunction with liabilities, notably bonds payable. Bonds are debt instruments issued by a corporation which have a face value, a stated interest rate to be paid on face, and a maturity date at which time the bonds will be redeemed at face value. As a short example, assume a bond with a face value of $10,000 is going to be sold to an investor on 1/1/2001. It pays 8% interest on face annually on Dec. 31, and it will mature in 3 years. If the going market rate of interest on like risk bonds is also 8%, the bond will sell at face value since investors can do no better elsewhere. However, if the market rate is higher than 8%, the 8% bond will sell at a discount to make it competitive with the market. In such a case, it is customary to use a Bond Discount contra account which is deducted from the face amount of the bond to show the present value of the bond, i.e., its value at the market rate of interest at the date of issuance. It is this present value which is recorded as the book value of the bond. The accounting will now be shown assuming the $10,000 bond described above was sold for $9,700, i.e., at a $300 discount.

1/1/01	**Bond issuance**		
	Dr: Cash	$9,700	
	Dr: Bond Discount (Bonds Payable reduction account) $300		
	Cr: Bonds Payable (face)		$10,000

If a balance sheet were prepared at this time, it would show:

Liabilities

Bonds Payable (face)	**$10,000**
Less Bond Discount	**(300)**
Bonds Payable (book value)	**$9,700**

12/31/01	**Interest is paid and one-year's discount amortized (i.e., written off)**[1]	
	Dr: Interest Expense	$900
	Cr: Bond Discount($^1/_3$ x $300)	$100
	Cr: Cash(.08 x $10,000 face)	$800

The credit of $100 to Bond Discount in the above entry increases the bond liability from its previous $9,700 to $9,800 by reducing the contra account as can be seen in the following balance sheet presentation at 12/31/01.

Liabilities

Bonds Payable (face)	**$10,000**
Less Bond Discount	**(200)**
Bonds Payable (book value)	**$9,800**

The 12/31/01 entry above will be repeated two times (at 12/31/02 and 12/31/03) and at the end of year 3, the Bond Discount account would be eliminated. At that time, the bonds would be

---

[1] The straight-line method of accounting for the write-off (amortization) of bond discount and premium will be used rather than the effective interest method. (This is permitted if the straight-line method gives results not materially different from those of the effective interest method).

redeemed and the following entry made.

Dr: Bonds Payable (face)	**$10,000**	
Cr: Cash		**$10,000**

In the above example, total interest expense over the life of the bond was $2,700 which consisted of 3 year-end cash payments of $800 each totaling $2,400 plus the $300 discount which was paid at maturity as part of the face value of the bond. By including $100 of the discount as additional interest each year, the total interest of $2,700 was spread at $900 per year over the 3 years during which the use of money service was received.

The counterpart to a contra account is an <u>adjunct</u> account which is an account <u>added</u> to a primary account to which it is related. To illustrate the use of an adjunct account, the same bonds payable example as above will be used but with the assumed market rate of interest now being lower than the corporation's bond rate of 8%. This would make the 8% bond more attractive than bonds of like risk and it would be sold at a premium, i.e., above face. The example which follows assumes the 8%, $10,000 face value bond was sold for $10,300. i.e., at $300 premium. A Bond Premium adjunct account will be used which is added to the face amount of the bond to show the present book value of the debt.

1/1/01 <u>**Bond issuance**</u>		
Dr: Cash	**$10,300**	
Cr: Bonds Payable (face)		**$10,000**
Cr: Bond Premium (Bonds Payable		**$300**
addition account)		

If a balance sheet were prepared at this time, it would show:

Liabilities	
Bonds Payable (face)	**$10,000**
Add Bond Premium	**$300**
Bonds Payable (book value)	**$10,300**

12/31/01 <u>**Interest is paid and one-year's premium amortized (i.e., written off)**</u>		
Dr: Interest Expense	**$700**	
Dr: Bond Premium($1/3$ x $300)	**$100**	
Cr: Cash (.08 x $10,000 Face)		**$800**

The debit of $100 to Bond Premium in the above entry decreases the bond liability from its previous $10,300 to $10,200 by reducing the adjunct account as can be seen in the following balance sheet presentation at 12/31/01.

Liabilities	
Bonds Payable (face)	$10,000
Add Bond Premium	$200
Bonds Payable (book value)	$10,200

The 12/31/01 entry above will be repeated two times (at 12/31/02 and 12/31/03) and, at the end of Year 3, the Bond Premium account would be eliminated. At that time the bonds would be redeemed and the following entry made.

Dr: Bonds Payable (face)	$10,000	
Cr: Cash		$10,000

In the above example, total interest expense over the life of the bond was $2,100 since only $700 of each of the 3 yearly payments of $800 was for interest. The additional $100 per year was a return of the bondholder's own money, i.e., the amount of premium paid. This is so because the bondholder, while paying $10,300 for the bond, will only receive the $10,000 face value at maturity.

Sometimes bonds are redeemed by the issuing corporation prior to maturity. If there is associated unamortized bond discount on the books the form of the redemption entry would be as follows:

Redemption of bonds with associated discount

Dr: Bonds Payable (face)
    Cr: Bond Discount (to eliminate its balance)
    Cr: Cash (amount paid)
Dr: Loss (to balance entry)
         OR
Cr: Gain (to balance entry)

If bonds with unamortized premium are redeemed prior to maturity, the form of the entry would be:

Redemption of bonds with associated premium

Dr: Bonds Payable (face)
Dr: Bond Premium (to eliminate its balance)
    Cr: Cash (amount paid)
Dr: Loss (to balance entry)
         OR
Cr: Gain (to balance entry)

Adjunct and contra accounts can also be found in the owners' equity section of the balance sheet. As an example, capital stock often has a par value which in some states is a legal requirement dealing with the price at which the stock can be sold and the amount of dividends which can be paid on it.[2] In such cases, accountants use the capital stock account to show the entity's obligation to stockholders for the par value part of their investment. In addition, an adjunct paid-in-capital in excess of the par account is used to show the entity's obligation to stockholders for the amount invested over par. The accounting is as follows for 1,000 shares of stock with a $50 par issued at $55 a share.

Stock issuance

Dr: Cash	$55,000	
Cr: Capital Stock (par)		$50,000
Cr: Paid-in-Capital in excess of par		$5,000
(Capital Stock addition account)		

The balance sheet presentation would be:

Owners' Equity

Capital Stock (par)	$50,000
Paid-in-Capital in excess of par	$5,000
Total	$55,000

The last example of this section involves a deficit which is a contra owners' equity account. To illustrate, assume a corporation with capital stock of $200,000 has a net income in its first year of operations of $60,000 and pays no dividends. The owners' equity section of the balance sheet at the end of that year would show:

Owners' Equity

Capital Stock	$200,000
Retained Earnings	60,000
Total Owners' Equity	$260,000

Now assume in the second year, the same corporation suffers a net loss of $70,000 which eliminates the $60,000 retained earnings and results in a negative deficit position of $10,000. The balance sheet presentation would be:

Owners' Equity

Capital Stock	$200,000
Less Deficit	(10,000)
Total Owners' Equity	$190,000

---

[2] Sometimes, "stated value" is used rather than "par value."

The deficit which is shown above as contra to capital stock means that the owners' invested assets have been eroded through operations to the extent of $10,000, and the entity's obligation to owners now stands at $190,000. Looking ahead to next year, the deficit could revert to a positive retained earnings if net income exceeds $10,000 or alternatively the deficit could grow if another net loss occurs.

Contractual Exchanges

After stressing the recording of exchanges throughout all the prior material, it may come as a surprise that some exchanges are not recorded in accounting. Contractual exchanges in which the entity and another party obligate themselves to each other are typically not recorded. An example would be a purchase contract between a customer and a supplier. Such exchanges are called "executory contracts" because the transfer of any cash or goods or service is yet to come, i.e., has yet to be executed.

As shown in the chart below, exchanges can be categorized into levels based on their degree of execution or performance on the part of the entity and the other party involved.

Levels of Exchange

Level	In the Exchange the Entity:	
	Receives	Gives
1. Executory Contract: No transfer of cash, goods or service as yet.	Claim against other party	Obligation to other party
2. Partially Executed:		
A. The entity has transferred cash, goods or service	Claim against other party	Cash, goods or service
or		or
B. The other party has transferred cash, goods or service	Cash, goods or service	Obligation to other party
3. Fully Executed: Both have transferred cash, goods or service	Cash, goods or service	Cash, goods or service

Because of the idea that nothing of real substance has been transferred in level 1 above, contemporary accounting does not record it and, therefore, the offsetting claim and obligation would not be shown in the entity's balance sheet. However, the contract would be disclosed in a footnote to the financial statements if the amount were significant. Levels 2 and 3 are of course recorded and would impact the financial statements.

Concluding Comments

Except for an appendix and two remaining final exercises, this brings to an end a brief yet fairly comprehensive exposure to the fundamentals of accounting. The objective was to impart an understanding of the logic and procedures of the double-entry accounting process and the financial statements resulting from it. Hopefully, this objective has been achieved, and the knowledge gained will prove beneficial. Good luck in using it in your academic and/or business endeavors.

Current Value Reporting

As a final note, accounting does in some limited instances deviate from the exchange-based procedures described in this book. What is typically done is to adjust the historical exchange-based book values of certain assets up or down to their current market values. In so doing, unrealized gains or losses are recorded prior to an actual exchange of the asset taking place. This of course does violate the exchange concept but it is sanctioned in some cases due to special circumstances.

Examples of circumstances warranting current value reporting would be the nature of the entity (e.g., a financial investment institution) or the account involved (e.g., short-term marketable securities). It is important to recognize that current value reporting does not invalidate the conventional exchange-based nature of accounting; it is simply an exception to the norm for pragmatic reasons.

Exercise 1 Journal Entries

For each of the statements below, make the required journal entry. (The effects of the journal entries on the financial statements are not required.)

Example: A $2,000 sale to a credit customer was made.

Dr: Accounts Receivable $2,000
     Cr: Sales Revenue $2,000

1. The credit customer in the example above remits promptly and a 3% cash discount is granted.

2. Estimated uncollectible accounts receivable in the amount of $5,000 are recorded.

3. A customer's $300 account receivable was written off as uncollectible.

4. Depreciation of $9,000 is recorded on equipment using an accumulated depreciation account.

5. The equipment in 4 above which cost $90,000 was sold for $26,000 cash. The balance in the accumulated depreciation account at the time of the sale was $54,000.

6. 10 year, 6% bonds payable with a face value of $100,000 are issued for $96,000 (i.e. at a $4,000 discount) and cash is collected.

7. The first annual payment is made on the bonds issued in 6 above and $400 discount is amortized as part of the interest entry.

8. The bonds issued is 6 above are redeemed prior to maturity at a price of $101,000. Unamortized discount on the books at the time of the redemption was $2,000.

9. 10 year, 7% bonds payable with a face value of $100,000 are issued for $104,000 (i.e. at a $4,000 premium) and cash is collected.

10. The first annual interest payment is made on the bonds issued in 9 above and $400 premium is amortized as part of the interest entry.

11. The bonds issued in 9 above are redeemed prior to maturity at a price of $101,000. Unamortized premium on the books at the time of the redemption was $2,000.

12. Bonds with a face value of $50,000 are redeemed at maturity after all interest has been paid and recorded.

13. Capital stock with a par value of $100,000 is issued for cash of $120,000.

14. A contract is signed to deliver goods in the future at a set price of $10,000.

Exercise 1 Solution

1. Dr: Cash $1,940
   Dr: Sales Discount $60
       Cr: Accounts Receivable $2,000

2. Dr: Uncollectible Accounts Expense $5,000
       Cr: Allowance for Uncollectible Accounts $5,000

3. Dr: Allowance for Uncollectible Accounts $300
       Cr: Accounts Receivable $300

4. Dr: Depreciation Expense $9,000
       Cr: Accumulated Depreciation $9,000

5. Dr: Cash $26,000
   Dr: Accumulated Depreciation $54,000
   Dr: Loss $10,000
       Cr: Equipment $90,000

6. Dr: Cash $96,000
   Dr: Bond Discount $4,000
       Cr: Bonds Payable $100,000

7. Dr: Interest Expense $6,400
       Cr: Bond Discount $400
       Cr: Cash (.06 x $100,000) $6,000

8. Dr: Bonds Payable $100,000
   Dr: Loss $3,000
       Cr: Bond Discount $2,000
       Cr: Cash $101,000

9. Dr: Cash $104,000
       Cr: Bonds Payable $100,000
       Cr: Bond Premium $4,000

10. Dr: Interest Expense $6,600
    Dr: Bond Premium $400
        Cr: Cash (.07 x $100,000) $7,000

11. Dr: Bonds Payable $100,000
    Dr: Bond Premium $2,000
        Cr: Cash $101,000
        Cr: Gain $1,000

12. Dr: Bonds Payable $50,000
    Cr: Cash $50,000

13. Dr: Cash $120,000
    Cr: Capital Stock $100,000
    Cr: Paid-in-Capital in excess of par $20,000

14. No entry is required since this is a contractual arrangement involving an offsetting claim and obligation.

Exercise 2 Balance Sheet with Contra and Adjunct Accounts

From the alphabetical list of accounts and their balances given below prepare a balance sheet. (Classification of accounts as current or long-term is not required.)

Accounts and Balances ('000 omitted)

Accounts Payable	$70
Accounts Receivable	130
Accumulated Depreciation: Equipment	50
Allowance for Uncollectible Accounts	20
Bond Discount (Class A)	10
Bonds Payable (Class A)	150
Bonds Payable (Class B)	100
Bond Premium (Class B)	20
Capital Stock (par)	400
Cash	120
Deficit	80
Equipment	300
Inventory	200
Investment in Bonds*	100
Paid-in-Capital in excess of par	120
Prepaid Rent Expense	20
Unearned Revenue	30

*This account is an asset showing that this company holds bonds of another company and has a receivable claim against that company. It is recorded by the following type of entry:

Dr: Investment in Bonds $100
    Cr: Cash $100

Exercise 2 Solution

Balance Sheet

Assets			Liabilities and Owner's Equity		
Cash		$120	**Liabilities:**		
Accounts Receivable	$130		Accounts Payable		$ 70
Less Allowance for			Unearned Revenue		30
Uncollectible Accts.	(20)		Bonds Payable (Class A)	$150	
Accounts Receivable(net)		110	Less Bond Discount		(10)
Inventory		200	Bonds Payable (net)		140
Prepaid Rent Expense		20	Bonds Payable (Class B)	$100	
Investment in Bonds		100	Add Bond Premium		20
Equipment	300		Bonds Payable(total)		120
Less Accumulated			Total Liabilities		360
Depreciation	(50)		**Owner's Equity:**		
Equipment (net)		250	Capital Stock (par)	$400	
			Paid-in-Capital in		
			Excess of par	120	
			Total	520	
			Less Deficit	(80)	
			Total Owner's Equity		$440
			Total Liabilities and		
Total Assets		$800	Owner's Equity		$800

End Notes
Works Referenced

[I] The idea of exchanges being recorded in accounting with the <u>debit</u> equating to <u>receive</u> and <u>credit</u> to <u>give</u> has been mentioned by several authors. Among these are A.C. Littleton, <u>Accounting Evolution to 1900</u>, American Institute Publishing Co., 1933; Breidenbaugh, Lins, Elwell <u>Bookkeeping Principles</u> (Toronto: Pitman Publishing Corp.) 1958, William J. Schrader, "An Inductive Approach to Accounting Theory," <u>The Accounting Review</u>, The American Accounting Association, October 1962, Schrader, Malcolm, Willingham, <u>Financial Accounting: An Events Approach</u> (Houston: Dame Publications, Inc.), 1981. Specific contributions of these writers will be acknowledged as they appear.

[II] Schrader, Malcolm, Willingham, <u>Financial Accounting, An Events Approach</u> (Houston: Dame Publications, Inc., 1981), p.4.

[III] Ralph C. Jones, "Some Aspects of Cost," <u>Accounting, Auditing, and Taxes</u>, AICPA, 1942 p. 104.

[IV] Schrader, "An Inductive Approach," p. 649.

[V] A.C. Littleton, <u>Structure of Accounting Theory</u>, (Sarasota: American Accounting Association, 1985) p.56

[VI] Jones, p. 104

[VII] Eldon S. Hendricksen, <u>Accounting Theory</u>, (New York: Richard D. Irwin, Inc. 1982) p. 173.

[VIII] Schrader, "An Inductive Approach," p. 648

[IX] William A. Paton, <u>Accounting Theory</u> (Chicago: Accounting Studies Press Ltd. 1962) chapters 2 and 3.

[X] Stephen Gilman, <u>Accounting Concepts of Profit</u> (New York: Ronald Press, 1939) p. 64.

[XI] Schrader, "An Inductive Approach," p. 647.

[XII] Schrader, "An Inductive Approach," p. 648

[XIII] Schrader, "An Inductive Approach" p. 649

[XIV] Francis A. Bird, Lewis F. Davidson and Charles H. Smith, "Perceptions of External Accounting Transfers Under Entity and Proprietary Theory," <u>The Accounting Review,</u> The American Accounting Association, July 1971.

Made in the USA
Lexington, KY
13 June 2014